Onigamiising

Onigamiising

SEASONS OF AN OJIBWE YEAR

LINDA LeGARDE GROVER

UNIVERSITY OF MINNESOTA PRESS

MINNEAPOLIS
LONDON

The essays in this book were originally published in the
Duluth Budgeteer.

Published by the University of Minnesota Press
111 Third Avenue South, Suite 290
Minneapolis, MN 55401-2520
http://www.upress.umn.edu

Library of Congress Cataloging-in-Publication Data

Grover, Linda LeGarde, author.
Onigamiising : seasons of an Ojibwe year / Linda LeGarde Grover.
Minneapolis : University of Minnesota Press, [2017] |
    ISBN 978-1-5179-0344-2 (pb)
Subjects: LCSH: Grover, Linda LeGarde. | Ojibwa Indians—
    Minnesota—Social life and customs. | Ojibwa philosophy. | Ojibwa
    women—Minnesota—Duluth—Biography. | Ojibwa Indians—Minnesota—
    Cultural assimilation. | Minnesota—
    Social life and customs. | Duluth (Minn.)—Biography.
Classification: LCC E99.C6 G76 2017 (print) | DDC 977.004/97333—dc23

LC record available at https://lccn.loc.gov/2017011653

Printed in the United States of America on acid-free paper

The University of Minnesota is an equal-opportunity
educator and employer.

27 26 25 24 23   11 10 9 8 7 6 5

To Onigamiising
with special love
for the West End

Contents

Here in Onigamiising

Noongoom mindimoye, niin. I am a grandmother now, a Nokomis, and an old-timer, an Ojibwe-ikwe who has lived three of her life's seasons here in Onigamiising—Ziigwan, Niibin, and Dagwaagin—and who has begun her fourth season, Biboon. These essays address both historical and contemporary life in northeast Minnesota from my perspective as an Ojibwe woman.

Spring to summer to fall to winter. The number four is significant to the Ojibwe people: there are four directions, four races of mankind, four seasons, and four sacred medicines. The short, reflective pieces in this book were written over the past decade or so; they have been saved in file folders, boxes, and on my computer hard drive. Collected and sorted on my front room floor, they seem to loosely follow the four seasons, the cycle that is the foundation of how the Ojibwe have lived for many generations. The Ojibwe of long ago followed that rhythm of the seasons in weather, lives, history, and in their physical and spiritual well-being for themselves and others. As each season of the year has beauty and value, so does each season of our own lives. We who live out the four seasons of life are fortunate and prayerfully appreciative of the gift: Ziigwan (Spring) is followed by Niibin (Summer), which is followed by Dagwaagin (Fall), and then our fourth season, Biboon (Winter). Our time on Mother Earth will end, we know, but we mindimooyag dash akiiwensii know that when our seasons have completed there is continuity beyond our existence as individuals. Biboon leads that greater life to what always follows, which is another spring and thus the continuation of the story.

Nindanakii Onigamiising. Onigamiising is the Ojibwe name for Duluth. In Ojibwe language vowels and consonants don't sound exactly the same as they do in English, but a fairly close pronunciation might be "AH nih gum AY sing." The word translates in English to "place of the small portage," most likely in reference to the Park Point peninsula, which Native people, voyageurs, and fur traders crossed overland by portage to shorten the journey between Lake Superior and the St. Louis River Bay.

I was born in Onigamiising, the place of the small portage, as were my parents, my brothers and sisters, my children, grandchildren, and many of my relatives by blood and endearment. My grandparents came here to Onigamiising from two different reservations, Fond du Lac and Bois Forte, more than a century ago. Today most of our large extended family lives here; the rest still call it home.

What is it about this place, this onigamiising? Why do we live here? Duluth is beautiful: stunningly, breathtakingly, sometimes even achingly, but a lifelong love requires more than a physical attraction. Our love of this place is more than the steepness of the hills with their startling assertions of rock, more than the big lake that changes color and surface under the skies of the seasons, more even than that spectacular variety of the four seasons, that number four so meaningful in the pattern and rhythm of timeless Ojibwe tradition.

A sense of place intertwines time, space, and purpose as well as reason for being. This place of the small portage was home to Ojibwe people who lived and walked here before Onigamiising was Duluth. Even longer ago than that, before the Great Ojibwe Migration from the East, it was home to other indigenous people who are long gone but whose spirits remain. Surely we sense this; surely we know that the essence of those spirits is a presence more real than the tangible in our lives every day in this beautiful place. To be a mindemoye nokomis in Duluth is to remember that one day it will be the same for us: where we walk, others will follow after we are no longer here. What we live today we will leave to those who will continue our Ojibwe ways here in Onigamiising, the place of the small portage.

Ziigwan

Spring

Spring Is Finally upon Us

*t*he Ojibwe word for spring is Ziigwan (SEE-gwon). Here in Onigamiising, spring arrived a little later this year than last (as it had the year before, come to think of it). It seemed as though winter had decided to stay on indefinitely those two years: right before the schools' spring break a blizzard closed down much of town, including the schools. At my house, the wind blew snow into a drift that nearly covered the back door (we had to go out through the front door to shovel), and yet because we were in the season of Ziigwan, the warming sun was out for a little longer each day, and each afternoon a little more ice and snow melted away. The morning after the second blizzard, an opiichii (oh-PEACHY, the Ojibwe word for robin), that sure sign of spring, sat on a snow-covered tree outside my sister Susie's kitchen window. She took its picture. Susie would have one more spring after that, before she left us, and the world, too, a sadder place.

It blizzarded again during the last two days of spring break that year. On our street, the storm kept the schoolchildren inside only until the wind quieted down, then they were out with their sleds, shovels, and dogs, enjoying themselves, each other, and the new snow. It took two days to get everyone plowed out, then it was back-to-school time.

Here in Onigamiising, approximately eight thousand students attend Duluth public schools. Of these, 650 or so are American Indian children. There are more than 850 teachers, including both full- and part-time; of these, a half-dozen or so are American Indian teachers.

I admire schoolteachers. Over the years I have taught many K-12 education majors at the University of Minnesota Duluth, in both education and American Indian studies classes. I find their motivation, humor, and can-do attitude touching. Education students are almost invariably creative and altruistic, qualities that they will carry into their teaching careers and their work with children. Most take postgraduate coursework and training throughout the span of their work lives to keep current and enhance their development as educators.

I admire American Indian teachers for the same reasons I do all teachers, as well as several more. They are a part of a time-honored trust that is integral to Mino-bimaadiziwin, which in Ojibwe language means the living of a good life. Mino-bimaadiziwin involves standards of behavior that include modesty, respect, thankfulness, generosity, and an awareness of one's ability and obligation to contribute to the well-being of others. In Ojibwe tribal traditions, teaching and learning have always been regarded as a natural and lifelong process: those who teach are highly respected and appreciated. In Ojibwe society everyone eventually teaches others, but the bedrock of teaching and with it the ultimate responsibility and honor have traditionally been entrusted to elders.

The passing of knowledge from one generation to another is the means by which we have survived as a people. Teaching is, at its heart, an act of generosity.

When I was a schoolchild here in Onigamiising, I never had an American Indian schoolteacher. It didn't occur to me that such a thing was even possible. These days I think sometimes about what it must mean to the students, and especially the Native students, to be taught by an American Indian schoolteacher.

I know every single one of that handful of American Indian teachers in the Duluth public schools. Some I met in class, some I have known since they were babies. Each of them has walked the good walk through school, through college, and through their job hunt, carrying our good wishes, our hopes, and our dreams. They carry this with them not only as they work in their classrooms but as they live their lives outside of school as well.

They also carry, as teachers and community members, a high school graduation rate for American Indian students that hovers below 50 percent—here and nationwide—and our collective schooling/educational history that has involved such difficulties as the Indian boarding school system and federal Indian education policies that provided an inferior academic program while damaging children, families, and communities.

The path of an American Indian teacher is not an easy one. Yet, as good Anishinaabeg they are aware of the positive contributions they can make to students, schools, Indian Country, and Onigamiising, so they walk their path with courage and grace.

My dad taught me long ago that the most important Ojibwe word to know is migwech (thank you). Recently I saw a bumper sticker that read, "If you can read this, thank a teacher!" I would like to take this opportunity to thank the teachers of Onigamiising, with a particular migwech to that handful of Anishinaabe gikinoo'amaagewiniwag, who make us so proud and give us hope. I hope that all of you had an enjoyable spring break, that you got plowed out in time to have some fun (after you finished shoveling), and that you returned to school rested and replenished for your important work.

Take good care of our precious children and of yourselves.

When the Sky Sings

*W*hen I was a little girl, I liked going outside on overcast spring and fall mornings because on some days, and I never knew which ones they would be, I could hear a comforting, melodically tuneless sound coming from the sky. This was a sort of low musical roar that seemed to change pitch every few seconds; I suppose that there is probably a scientific explanation having to do with laws of physics and air pressure and barometer and humidity.

As I grew closer to adulthood I was able to hear the sky's morning song less often. I suppose that there must be some scientific explanation for this also, perhaps that children's ears are physically more sensitive to the vibrations that are sound.

Science can explain many things, but not necessarily everything.

When we are born, we are placed upon the Earth by the Creator, who has for each of us a purpose and destiny;

in that way we are like Nanaboozhoo, whose adventures and decisions affected so much of how the world came to be the way it is, and why things are the way they are. There is something of Nanaboozhoo in every one of us, I think. When we leave for the next world, what will be the legacies of our own adventures and decisions? I wonder. When I was a child my wonderings were not like this yet. Children's tasks, set by the Creator, are different from ours; the jobs they have to do will change as they grow into adulthood and then elderhood.

Here is what I think: the singing of the sky was a magical gift of the Creator, perhaps a special spring and fall seasonal blessing given especially for children. The minds, hearts, and spirits of children, newer to Earth than ours, have been created with a purity that is the strength of childhood and the foundation of human existence. As we experience life we learn many things; that, too, is the plan and intent of the Creator. We move through adventures that fill our minds, hearts, and spirits with human knowledge that is limited and imperfect; because there are things we simply cannot know, we become less comfortable with the unknown. A child who is visited by the little people or spirits has not learned to be frightened by the unfamiliar or unearthly; an adult has learned to be.

What is the reason and purpose behind the tuneless, comforting melody of the sky's song? I have not yet been able to give as much thought to the Dagwaagin song as I have to the Ziigwan; the unknown of fall-to-winter in life's seasons is just a little too unsettling at this point in my journey. And so until the time that my own spirit begins its way back to the beginnings and the childhood purity that will be the strength that gives courage to the ending of our time on Earth, I will think about the sky song of spring.

Here in Onigamiising, every year when March comes along we watch for signs of Ziigwan; after all, the first official day of spring is around March 21. We wake in the morning to a sky that since the fall equinox has lightened minutes earlier than the day before; we watch for snowbanks to decrease in size. Although some of the biggest storms have come to Onigamiising during the month of March, we know from experience that the steadily increasing minutes of daylight and temperatures mean that spring is on its way. We can feel it; if we listen in the way that children do, can we hear it in the sky?

When I look up at the sky on overcast mornings I occasionally hear it, and for a moment I am a child again. I greet the sky with a song we used to sing in elementary school joined by the child who still lives in my spirit, before getting into the car for the drive to work:

> *In March when we hear the wind blowing*
> *sometimes it whistles a tune;*
> *it tells us cold weather is going,*
> *and spring will be here very soon.*

Over the years, because I hear the sky song less and less often, it is all the more precious every time that I do. And when I see children walking to school or waiting for the bus on overcast mornings, I wish them many blessings from the Creator and wonder if today might be one of the days that they hear the sky singing, themselves.

Minikwe niibish,
the Leaf We Drink

*T*he word for tea in Ojibwe is niibish, which also means
leaf. Niibish is pronounced NEE-bish; an Anglicized
version I have also heard is Ni-tih (nih-TIH). Traditionally, the Ojibwe made teas from the leaves, berries,
barks, and roots of the plants, grasses, and trees that the
Creator has provided for our use during the time we
spend on Earth. Some teas are liked for their flavor or
color; raspberry has long been an Ojibwe favorite, hot
or cold. Some are medicinal, for colds, fevers, stomach
ailments, to ease childbirth, to strengthen mind, body,
or spirit. There are some teas brewed from ingredients
known only to the healers who mix them.

Evenings, when I was a girl, my dad and I often sat
at the kitchen table reading, playing cribbage or chess,
talking with my mother, enjoying the activity of my
thirteen younger brothers and sisters coming and going
through the kitchen, and drinking tea. Our house was

full of not just family but also friends and relatives, who we treated with old-fashioned manners: visitors were offered a place to sit, something to eat, and coffee or tea. My mother drank Arco coffee with milk and sugar, my dad Lipton tea; their relatives and friends seemed to share their preferences. We, my dad and I, took our tea with sugar and sometimes a little ReaLemon juice, and we shared a teabag, which was good for two or three cups.

A visitor surprised us once by adding milk to his tea, which he poured into the saucer to cool; then he lifted the saucer like a bowl and drank (it took some self-control for us kids to not stare, since well-mannered Ojibwe children are taught to not show surprise at anything a guest might do).

When we lived in the country, our water came from a well that froze in the middle of winter and went dry in the middle of summer. During those times our drinking water came from our grandparents' house, in rinsed-out milk cartons; we used it carefully, without squandering. One cold winter afternoon I asked my dad if he would like some tea. To conserve water I used the leftover from a saucepan of hot dogs I had just boiled up for lunch. I can still see the look on his face when he took a sip of that tea. "[Pause] . . . what kind of water is this?" "Wiener water."

Sometimes I was allowed to make the tea for company, which I loved. One day my Uncle Ray brought a new tea for us to try. He took a small tin out of his jacket pocket and pried open the round lid with his pocketknife. He explained that this tea didn't come in bags but brewed at the bottom of the saucepan. It smelled lovely; small dimpled yellow ovals among dark red-brown leaves looked exotic. "What are those little things?" "Callouses." I peeked at him sideways and made the tea. He said to be sure to stir in a little sugar, and the tea would taste like oranges growing in heaven. He was right. That tea, Constant Comment, was heavenly, and today, more than a half-century later, when we drink it we think of our uncle.

I have a lot of tea at my house, some in a Lipton box and some in little cardboard boxes with fanciful pictures: the teabags inside are wrapped in their own little colored packets. I love it all. Sometimes when I visit my mother I bring along tea, not because she needs it (she keeps an assortment of teabags in a large jar on the kitchen counter) but because in bringing that little box or handful of packets I bring the past: our past; my dad, Uncle Ray, and sugared tea that tasted like the oranges that grow in heaven, where they both live now; a saucer of milk tea held by two hands like a chalice; my dad's eyebrows raising so comically at that taste of wiener-water tea; my mother lifting a saucepan of boiling water off the hot stove with an oven mitt; my brothers and sisters trying tea out as they became old enough.

My sister Nancy called me one night not long ago and said that she was thinking of me. She was going over some old photographs and found one of me and our dad sitting at the kitchen table drinking tea. Did I remember that? she asked. She knew, of course, that I did.

Onishishin

IT'S ALL PRETTY, IT'S ALL GOOD

The lovely and assuring Ojibwe word onishishin translates literally into English as "That's pretty," but it has meaning and implication far beyond the literal. I believe this is due to differences in cultural points of reference and shades of meaning, both in language and in how the world is viewed. Those differences are, to me, sometimes funny and sometimes poignant but always endearing and interesting.

I have heard the statement that something is pretty made in both the English language and Ojibwemowin. Most of the time it has been spoken by an older person. Onishishin or "That's pretty" can apply to an attractive sight, a way of behaving, or something that is right or good, something that is nice. In either language the phrase grounds the comment or compliment in Ojibwe tradition and worldview.

How might this term be used in Ojibwemowin or English conversation, and what does it really mean, beyond the simple translation?

One example could be a sunset. We all notice and remark on this from time to time. On an evening that my husband, Tim, and I were pulling into the Kmart parking lot to buy a jar of instant coffee and a get-well card, the orange brilliance of the setting sun offsetting heavy-looking pink and purple clouds filled the western end of the sky.

"Do you see that? Isn't that something?" Tim commented.

It was something, indeed. To the east the sky was a dusty denim blue that grew darker as rain approached. Ahead, behind the BigK sign, the color of the sun deepened to a dark red-orange sinking weightily into the purple clouds, outlining them in gold. What an ending to a beautiful day: our grandchildren had spent the afternoon playing at our house. We were listening to music on the radio. There was half a carton of strawberry ice cream in the freezer at home.

"It's pretty, isn't it?" I answered.

Onishishin.

A few years ago, a woman I know worked very hard on a small community powwow that was held at Trepanier Hall, downtown on Second Street. Because she was willing to do so much, I am a little embarrassed to say that the rest of us didn't really work as hard as we might have. She had coordinated the event and taken care of the logistics of reserving the hall, inviting the drum, and contacting special guests, and she hoped very much that we would all remember to bring something for the potluck feast beforehand.

The powwow was a great success, a fun and pleasant evening. When the doors opened, the hall filled quickly, as did the tables of food. She greeted each and every person as they placed their food on the tables: hotdishes, cold cuts, cheese, wild rice, frybread, Jello salads, cookies, and more. (I, being a little short on time, brought a bucket of Kentucky Fried Chicken, which she acknowledged as admiringly as if I had cooked it myself.)

"What a nice powwow," an elder lady friend complimented her, "and everybody is having such a nice time. You did a good job. Onishishin."

A good Anishinaabikwe, that hardworking woman thanked us in return and quickly credited other people's contributions.

Onishishin. That was pretty.

When I was in my thirties, I went to college and took an Indian Studies class. We Native students sat in the front row: a young Dakota mother, an older Ojibwe man who had been one of the original American Indian Movement (AIM) members, and me.

We enjoyed ourselves hugely, soaking up Native history and the indigenous atmosphere, encouraging one another and even sometimes sharing something we knew with the rest of the class. We became so comfortable that the young mother offered to speak in front of the class about growing up on a reservation in South Dakota. She spoke simply and seriously of vast open spaces and the Badlands, of feasts and camping, of the preparation of those traditional Dakota foods waasna (a nutritious meat-and-berry dish) and wojapi (blue-berry pudding), of her school days and her grandfather's horses. She missed home, she said; she would return there when she finished school. When she had finished, she thanked us for listening and told us that she had wanted us to know this.

After class the AIM warrior said to her, "Thank you; that was pretty. Do you know what I mean when I say it was pretty? It means that what you said was nice, that it was just right. The old people used to say that."

Onishishin.

Curtains, Calico,
and Creative Living

*P*eople who like to sew usually have a fabric stash, which is a collection of lengths of material that they keep on hand for projects. My fabric stash, which is not as large as some, fits on four shelves of a wicker bookcase. Most of my fabric is floral or figured cotton that would work well for aprons or small quilts. Although each piece is folded into a (more or less) neat square, not all of it is brand-new. Unfolded, some pieces take on their original shapes and appearances: my husband's old cotton shirts, an out-of-style skirt, a set of curtains that my sister Gail used to have in her kitchen. Gail made them herself, of a cotton blue-green paisley print.

Although I am not using them anymore, I have a new plan for those curtains. With a little creative application on my part, they will make a nice apron and perhaps a pair of matching hot pads. When I give these to Gail as a little gift, her curtains will return to her, then, in a new form!

There can be a lot of enjoyment and satisfaction in the making and remaking of things. I can remember how, when I was a little girl, the relatives so appreciated the quilts that my great-grandmother made from old, discarded men's wool shirts and pants. The quilts were filled with cotton batting, and one layer was warm enough on the coldest of winter nights. Before our parents turned the lights out, we played games on the squares; the variety of fabrics and colors seemed endless. Great-grandmother made fabric dolls, too, with yarn hair and embroidered faces. The dolls were dressed in handmade outfits as endlessly varied as the squares of her quilts.

Like so many of the women in our family, my mother inherited that knack for making, remaking, and makeovers. As a kindergartner, one of my favorite things to wear was an ankle-length lacy nightgown, cut down from one of her own. Swishing around the house during the day I was a fairy; at bedtime I was a princess. When I outgrew a coat that I just loved (a striking shade of teal/turquoise wool), she lengthened the sleeves, shortened the hem, and turned it into a jacket. And when the May weather turned unexpectedly cold for the Denfeld prom, she bought a lace curtain for a dollar (!) and within a half-hour had cut and stitched it into a shawl!

My cousin Bob is an Ojibwe elder of many experiences and stories from reservation and town. Bob remembers well our family's arts and crafts stand up on old Highway 61. Our grandparents' generation made and sold beadwork, baskets, birchbark work, dolls, and artwork at the stand. Some of the materials that went into these came from the woods (willow branches, moss, rocks, birchbark). Some materials were purchased or traded for (beads). Some were from society's castoffs: rags became dolls and quilts; tin from cans and rubber from old inner tubes became foundations and backings of jewelry and toys.

It is the traditional and time-honored way of the Ojibwe to make good use of the gifts that life gives us. That is one of the ways in which we express our thanks and live the good life: Bimaadiziiwin. In looking at and making use of objects in new ways, we continue that Anishinaabe tradition and worldview. Cousin Bob calls it "creative living."

I believe that creative living is a form of art in itself, and that it is for everyone. It is healthy for the mind, body, and spirit as well as for the world we live in. And, as Bob says, it's fun.

A Wedding Shower
and a Four-Year-Old Girl

*t*he bride-to-be wore a nice dress. She was bright-eyed and pink-cheeked, and very excited and happy to be at a shower held in her honor. To welcome this newest member and her mother, sister, and friends into our extended family, we aunts and cousins had made treats, both sweet and savory, prepared to look as pretty as we could make them.

We brought chicken salad tarts, petits fours, a green salad, breads, and dips. My sister Gail had spent that afternoon piping filling into cherry tomatoes that she garnished with tiny leaves and presented on frilly confectionary papers; her daughter, my niece Julie, had done something similar with several dozen chocolate candy dainties topped with pale green mints. The table, with all those plates of jewel-like treats, looked lovely.

The youngest guest was a four-year-old girl, my sister Jeanne's granddaughter. She wore a nice dress, too, and was in charge of giving out the flower-topped pens for the shower games, which she did with a shy, big smile. Then she sat on the floor, between the long legs of a teenage cousin, to watch the guest of honor and the festivities.

The little sweetheart clearly enjoyed herself, and the privilege of being up past bedtime for an evening occasion with the big girls and ladies. She was taking it all in, watching everything and occasionally turning her head to see how her older cousin reacted to a joke, a prettily wrapped gift, or a sidebar conversation between a cheerfully kind aunt and the engaged girl, whose husband would be leaving for an overseas military deployment soon after the wedding.

My mother, Patsy, grandmother of the groom-to-be, was at the wedding shower, of course, and so were her sisters Peggy and Mary. When I was a little girl I spent quite a bit of time in the company of my mother and aunts as well as many other female relatives, and the fun my grandniece was having reminded me of those days. In a group of our size we have had a lot of showers for brides, expectant mothers, and an occasional anniversary or housewarming.

Over the years we women present at these gatherings have progressed through the passages of life here on Earth. When I attended my mother's baby shower as an unborn mystery, she, Peggy, and Mary were in their teens; since then, other women in our families have been born, had showers for their own weddings and babies, have grown older, and have passed on. We miss those ladies who are no longer among the living;

we take joy as little girls grow into women and roles of honor and responsibility.

Children learn a great deal by watching the people around them. As a child I, like my grandniece and other girls, was given the gift of learning by studying the people around me. At home, at relatives', at the grocery store, the library, at church, I observed and listened, thought things over, and then tried things out for myself. These are the first three steps of the Ojibwe tradition, which is the foundation of teaching and learning in cultures all over the world: intake of information, reflection, experience. The fourth step is when the learner, with practice and ability, becomes the teacher, who in turn is observed by those who will walk in those same footsteps.

What did that little four-year-old girl, who in the company of women at a social occasion was allowed to participate and stay up past bedtime, learn that evening? We, her female relatives and friends, cannot of course know for sure exactly what she thinks about what she sees, but I remember well how I felt when as a little girl I was allowed the privilege of attending and, especially, helping at one of our gatherings. To paraphrase from Dorothy Law Nolte's inspirational poem, children do, indeed, learn what they live.

Sewing Ojibwe Ribbon Skirts
in Onigamiising

*h*ere in Onigamiising, the Indian Education program staff and Parent Committee recently hosted get-togethers at which girls and women made ribbon skirts. Because I enjoy sewing, my daughter invited me to join the group. Because I am lady friends with my sewing machine, a Husqvarna named Lena, I brought her along, also.

The skirt-sewing gatherings began with refreshments and socializing, and then a little explanation about ribbon skirts: where they are worn and how they are sewn. One of the women had brought in some of her own pretty skirts as examples of how to measure for size, ideas for placement of ribbon, and sewing hints for stitching of the ribbon, the back seam, and the casing for the elastic waist.

Then we were ready to go! Some others besides me also brought their sewing machines, which we put to good work. Most of the skirts were made by young teenage girls, who were fascinated with the colors and patterns of the fabrics, with the choosing of ribbons to coordinate with the material, and the placement of the ribbons on the skirts. Although the basic design of the skirt was pretty simple, there was quite a bit of work to putting everything together; those of us with some sewing experience were happy to help and to share what we knew. The room became a very busy place: there were people working on all different stages of sewing their skirts, admiring each other's color combination choices, and chatting.

I worked closely with a young lady whose mother and grandmother I have known for some years. She chose a blue-green patterned fabric and then four ribbons, some wide and some narrow, in blue-green and shades of purple. How carefully she measured and cut, and how carefully she placed the ribbons in stripes, comparing different arrangements of color and size. When we had stitched much of the skirt together, she held it against herself to see how it would look when we added the waist casing and elastic. She and her mother looked proud and shy when I told her how beautiful she looked, which was certainly true. When she wears it, she will remember the skirt-making gathering of women from their early teens to elderhood; when I see her wearing it, I will think of the fun we had and will know that it was an honor to be part of continuing the ribbon skirt tradition for another generation.

Ribbon skirts, dresses, and shirts have been around in the Onigamiising area for several hundred years, since the arrival of the fur traders. Before the fur trade, Ojibwe clothing was made of soft, durable hide, stitched together with sinew lacing. Wool blankets and stroud cloth, flower-printed calico, needles and thread were among the many items that were brought here from Europe by the traders for exchange for processed pelts. Because fabric clothing could be made much more quickly and easily than buckskin, and because fabric is made in a variety of colors and prints, Ojibwe people integrated cotton and wool into their clothing (many people do still wear buckskin as part of traditional clothing today). The dresses, skirts, and shirts were sometimes decorated with ribbons or colored twill tape.

In the inner stairway at the Duluth Depot, on the way to the Ojibwe Gallery, there is a dress on display from the St. Louis County Historical Society's collections. The fabric is a dark-blue wool, perhaps originally a blanket, with colored tape trim. (That same dress can be seen in the Eastman Johnson painting *Hiawatha* right upstairs in the Ojibwe Gallery exhibit.) This dress is from Grand Portage, from the days of the fur trade, and is a grandmother to today's ribbon dresses and skirts. The top is folded over to make a sort of ruffle across the chest (many dresses made of blankets had this fold-over, called the "rainbow" because of the stripes); the ruffle and bottom of the skirt are trimmed with colored twill tape.

The dress is a color similar to my ribbon skirt, made in the 1980s. My skirt is cut a little fuller and is a little shorter than the skirts we have been sewing in the Indian Education gatherings (styles do change!), with a

pleated waist and matching leggings. The skirt and leggings are trimmed with red ribbons. Perhaps I will bring
it along to our next sewing get-together and show it to
the girls. I wonder if it will look a little old-fashioned
to them, and if they will feel a sense of wonder that
the skirt, decades older than they are, connects them
to generations of Ojibwe women who have sewn and
worn this same style of clothing.

The Ojibwe Word
for Moccasin Is . . .

. . . moccasin.

Moccasins are the soft leather footwear made and worn by the nearly five hundred different tribes of North America. The style and decoration of each tribe's moccasin reflect and represent cultural beliefs and values as well as the weather, terrain of the countryside, and resources available from the environment. There are differences between the moccasin style of the Blackfeet and that of the Pima, between that of the Dakota and that of the Ojibwe.

The classic Ojibwe moccasin design has a puckered, or gathered, seam where the sole is attached to the vamp, around the toes; I have heard that the root of the word *Ojibwe* refers to that puckered seam. Ojibwe *moccasinan* are usually made of deer or moose hide (the smoky scent of hand-tanned hide is one of my favorite smells) in three pieces: sole, vamp, and cuff. Many years ago, Ojibwe moccasins were decorated with porcupine quillwork; occasionally they still are. Glass beads manufactured in Europe were brought to North America by the fur traders; Native people, including the Ojibwe, adapted beads and other trade goods into everyday life. Beadwork was integrated into traditional arts, including the Ojibwe acknowledgment of living plants that can be seen on the Ojibwe moccasins.

On the vamp of many Ojibwe moccasins, both men's and women's, are beaded designs of flowers, vines, and leaves. Those floral patterns are more than just decoration: they have been put there to remind us of the living plants, flowers, and foliage that we walk on as we make our way through life on Earth. Underfoot, those flowers and plants give of themselves to support us on our journey; the beadwork on our moccasins makes us aware of that, and appreciative. To my mind, walking or dancing in moccasins is prayer of acknowledgment and thanks.

The collars and vamps of some Ojibwe moccasins are made of black velvet or thick heavy wool; some cuffs are edged with colored ribbon or tape trim. Like beads, ribbon and woven fabrics were brought here during the fur trade days, and the Ojibwe adapted them, as they did with beads, to our own ways and worldview. Although not as durable as leather, fabric has its advantages: beadwork embroidery can be done more easily and intricately on the softness of velveteen or wool, which can also be used again. When the leather sole wears out, the moccasins can be taken apart and the

beaded vamps and cuffs sewn onto a new sole to become part of a new pair.

Except for a baby itself, I can think of few things
cuter and more precious than a pair of baby moccasins.
It has been a while since I have made a pair; the task is
a labor of love and does take some time. And strong,
flexible fingers. I would have liked to make moccasins for my mother, but I have not mastered making
adult moccasins and so bought her a pair that I saw
when I was in Grand Portage. They have gold woolen
vamps with pink beaded curving flowers; the hide is
tanned to a lovely butternut, and the leather cuffs are
fringed. I bought them for my mother because they are
the happiest-looking moccasins I have seen; they made
me think of her. She keeps them by a chair in the front
room and wears them while she reads.

If you are not familiar with Ojibwe moccasins, the
next time you are at a powwow you might take a (politely indirect is how the Ojibwe do it) look at the
moccasins that the dancers are wearing. Some will be
wearing Ojibwe-style moccasins, some will be wearing
styles from other tribes. If the powwow is indoors, on a
hard concrete floor, some might wear tennis or athletic
shoes; I have known dancers who wear Dr. Scholl's
arch supports inside their moccasins. You will see babies and little children in moccasins elaborately and
lovingly decorated by their grandmothers, old men in
moccasins that they have taken special care of for years,
teenage girls in moccasins almost completely covered
with beadwork and whose feet prance like young deer

in springtime. You might see someone in canvas tennies beaded with Ojibwe-style leaves, flowers, and vines, an adaptation of Native tradition to modern shoes.

Watch the dancers and their moccasins politely and respectfully. And when the announcer says, "Inter-tribal time, nii-mii-ok! Everybody dance!" that is an invitation. At intertribal time, whether you are wearing moccasins or not, you are welcome to join the dancers inside the powwow circle.

Reservations, Homelands, and Extended Family Ties

*R*ecently a student in an American Indian studies class that I teach asked me, "What exactly is an Indian reservation?" He had never been on one, he said, but had seen signs on the highway that indicated when cars were entering the Grand Portage and Fond du Lac reservations. Were there boundaries? he wondered. And what did that mean?

I thought his question was a good one.

Here in Onigamiising, the place of the small portage, we live within driving distance to several reservations in both Minnesota and Wisconsin. The closest is Fond du Lac, which is less than a half-hour away. Fond du Lac covers a large area, from Brookston in the northeast to Sawyer in the southwest, and is crossed by many roads; it is not unlikely that the student who asked what a reservation is had been on and off reservation lands many times without even realizing it.

Yes, I told the student, there are reservation boundaries, and within those boundaries our tribal governments do govern and practice self-regulation according
to tribal constitutions and agreed-upon laws and terms
recorded in land acquisition treaties.

All over the United States, Indian reservations were
established by a series of treaties, most during the nineteenth century, that were negotiated between two sovereign bodies: Indian tribes and federal or state governments. Although both bodies participated in the
process, the tribes were at a disadvantage in that the
purpose of land acquisition treaties was the takeover of
vast tracts of land by what was a more powerful entity,
during a period of great destruction and loss. Under
those treaties, Indian tribes reluctantly agreed to cede,
or sign away, those vast areas of land. In return, our
ancestors negotiated terms that included such things as
payment for the land (held in trust, with some monies
distributed in small, short-term annuities), household
items (tools, plows, food commodities, seed, fabric),
and a much smaller area of land that would be reserved,
or set aside, for the tribe and ceded back once the treaties were finalized.

Those lands that were reserved and then ceded back
to the tribes are the reservations.

In 1936, six of the seven Ojibwe bands of northern
Minnesota incorporated to form the Minnesota Chippewa Tribe. They are Bois Forte (Nett Lake, Vermilion Lake), Grand Portage, Fond du Lac, White Earth,
Leech Lake, and Mille Lacs. The reservation boundaries have existed since the treaties were signed during

the nineteenth century and stand today. Within, our tribes retain certain rights to self-govern; they continue to exist as sovereign nations within the United States of America. The governance of the Minnesota Chippewa Tribe nations differs slightly from that of the seventh Ojibwe reservation, Red Lake.

The Red Lake Nation, in northwest Minnesota, did not incorporate into the Minnesota Chippewa Tribe. Red Lake never ceded what is now its reservation land during treaty negotiations; instead, they retained that land base. This might look like a fine point, but the legal ramifications of their always having owned the land that is the Red Lake Nation reservation have meant that the band has retained a degree of sovereignty and self-governance beyond that of nearly every tribe in the country. They remain a separate tribal government, proudly and justifiably so.

Today, it is not inappropriate, and in some situations is even good-mannered, for one Native person to ask another, "Where are you from?" (For older people, like myself, this might be followed by ". . . and who is your family?") The person asked will usually respond with the name of their reservation. (Of course, we must keep in mind that our history of displacements, disruptions, and adoptions might mean that a person wouldn't know, and so we try to be tactful and kind.) Whether one is a member of a band, or a direct descendant, the reservation one's family is from has become a part of not only one's legal status as an American Indian but an integral part of one's culture, history, and extended family as well.

During the great land losses of the treaty-making era of history, our ancestors demonstrated their wisdom and concern for future generations by negotiating treaty terms that still stand today. They stayed true to their own human dignity and ours, doing their best to ensure our survival as a people who would honor their struggles by doing our best to remember and live in ways that continue Mino-bimaadiziwin, the good life. Present in the treaties, in and between the lines, is the determination that future generations would survive. The result was that although during the times of the treaties American Indians lost almost all of their land base, the tribes retained legal identity, which is the foundation of today's tribal sovereignty and self-determination. This strengthens our even more important cultural and spiritual identity, all that makes us Anishinaabe.

It is all because of our ancestors. Onishishin.

To Catch
a Baby's Dream

*d*reamcatchers have been around for quite some time, longer than Duluth, longer than Onigamiising.

The Ojibwe story of the dreamcatcher is from the days long ago when all earthly creatures, human and otherwise, could communicate. Many stories begin with "Mewinzhaa, a long time ago when the animals and people could talk to each other . . ." Because the story of how the dreamcatcher came to be is one of the sacred creation stories, I believe that they should always be crafted with consideration and respect for the significance and lessons of the story in mind. And with a spiritual sense of prayer, of course, since the story comes from Ojibwe spirituality.

The story is an old one, passed down for generations within Ojibwe communities and families. It is the nature of the oral tradition that in the telling of stories certain elements are included by some families and

not others. This gives a regional distinction that can be
identified in the hearing of the stories and reflects the
care and discipline of the storykeeper/teller.

The way I have heard the story goes like this: long
ago, a mother wrapped and secured her baby in a cradleboard and brought it out into the woods, where she
leaned it against a tree trunk while she worked. When
it could not see her, the baby became bored and lonely
and a little frightened; it began to cry. A curious spider crawled down the tree trunk and onto the top of
the cradleboard, the curved bentwood roll bar there to
protect the baby's face and head, to see what was going
on. She spoke to the baby, "Don't cry, little one; your
mother will come back," but the baby continued to
fret and didn't hear. The spider then waved her front
legs back and forth to distract the crying baby, who was
tired but too uneasy to sleep. "What to do, what to
do?" the spider began to fret, herself; her fretsome legs
tangled the fine line of silk that she had been spinning
into a trap to catch her dinner when the baby's crying
had distracted her. Seeing how the silk caught the woven pattern in the sunlight, the spider waved a bit of it
in front of the baby, catching its interest and attention.
Ah, then the spider thought of what to do: she wove
a web that provided something pretty and interesting
for the baby to look at while awake, but that also protected the baby while it was asleep. The web was of an
intricate pattern that captured and contained the baby's
good dreams and thoughts; the pattern confused and
chased away any bad dreams that might fly through the

air in search of the sweet defenseless innocence of baby sleep. In the center of the web was a small hole; the pattern dazzled any bad dreams inside and tricked them into leaving through that Anishinaabeg.

After that, the Anishinaabeg began to make dream-catchers that they tied to cradleboards or above where little children slept. Eventually, dreamcatchers and the goodness connected to them spread far beyond the Ojibwe nation.

Spiders are industrious little creatures: they look so delicate to me, and it takes them a long time to spin and weave their lacy webs, which they must do for their own survival. The dreamcatcher was a gift of kindness from the spider, who took time from its own busy life to use its abilities to protect and care for a little being in need of its help. In doing so, the spider gave the Ani-shinaabe people something that we could imitate, both in the making of the object and in the remembering to watch out and care for others.

I love the dreamcatcher made by my niece Marlene when she was a little girl. She picked a supple and ten-der piece of red willow branch and, with her moth-er's help, tied it into a circle and wove a seven-spoked spiderweb of waxed linen thread. Into the design she worked two small, irregular turquoise beads the color of the sky; to the top she tied a small loop of turquoise-colored leather; to the bottom she knotted two strips of that same leather to which she tied four tiny feath-ers. And in the center, of course, she left a small hole. Marlene is a wife and mother herself now, but when I look at the dreamcatcher she made just for me, I picture a little girl, delicate and industrious as a spider, learning something from her mother that she would one day teach to her own children. Onishishin; that is how mino-bimaadiziwin, the good life, has survived to this day, and how it will continue to exist.

"What's a Hanky For?"

*d*uring this end-of-the-school-year season we relatives and friends of students have the pleasure of attending many enjoyable concerts, programs, and graduations. I have watched and listened to little children singing and older kids playing musical instruments; a granddaughter was promoted from middle to high school; a happy grandson graduated from Denfeld, from where, among other relatives, his father, grandfather, and great-grandfather graduated. As he walked across the stage to receive his diploma, I held a handkerchief in my hand, ready to dab at my eyes if I needed to. As it turned out I didn't; dry-eyed and proud I watched him walk across the same stage as I did when I too was a seventeen-year-old graduating senior.

Although I didn't use it at the Denfeld graduation, a handkerchief is a useful thing to have, and I usually keep a couple folded in my purse. You never know when

it will come in handy. At the St. James School spring
band concert/piano recital, one of my elementary-age
nieces came to sit next to me. She listened carefully
and politely to the music. I thought, "Such lovely manners; she is certainly growing into a young lady." In
my unzipped purse, at the top of the jumble inside,
were two folded, ironed handkerchiefs. I offered one
to my niece. "Would you like a hanky?" I whispered.

"Thank you," she whispered back and looked at the
piece of folded floral fabric. "It's pretty." She unfolded
the handkerchief, looked at the pink roses in each
corner, folded it back into a triangle shape. "What's a
hanky for?"

"Well, you can wipe your nose with it, instead of
Kleenex; if you splash a little of your milk while you are
eating, you can soak it up; if you get food on your face,
you can wipe it off."

"It's like a reusable napkin!" she whispered brightly.

My husband turned to see what we were doing; she
dabbed her hanky on her upper lip and smiled sweetly
at him. Then the young lady, conscious that she must
be a good example and role model for her auntie and
uncle, turned her attention again to the concert.

I don't know how many people still carry a handkerchief. I have two or three dozen, some that I use
every day, some that are too good to use, and some
that I keep for gifts. When I got home after the concert, I took the too-good and for-gifts hankies out of
the shoebox I keep them in and laid them out on the
kitchen table. Those hankies bring to my mind my
mother and my aunts, and other female relatives from

the days when I was a little girl, some of them long gone from this Earth.

When I was a little girl it seemed that every woman carried a handkerchief: in their purses or pockets; tucked into their sleeves; fan-folded and pinned to the bosom; flat-folded at their waists over a belt. Most of the women I knew carried decorated handkerchiefs, even for everyday use. Some of their hankies were lace-edged, some with flowers or monograms embroidered in the corners. Some were printed with designs of flowers, leaves, kittens, dogs.

My sixth-grade teacher used to have surprise inspections ("Did you bring a handkerchief to school?") that I learned to stay ahead of by keeping a couple of my dad's plain white ones at the back corner of my desk; my mother's pretty hankies were too nice for the darkness behind my textbooks and pencils.

Like the mothers of other kids, mine used to knot my milk money into the corner of a hanky; at school the teachers untied each child's knotted hanky, counted and recorded the coins, and handed the handkerchief back. And like other mothers, mine, when we were out and about and our faces became smeared or dirty, would whip that hanky from her purse/pocket/sleeve, say "Stick out your tongue," dab the hanky on our tongues, and wipe that smudge or bit of food right off!

"What's a hanky for?" Noses, hands, faces. Spills. Milk money. Decoration. Gifts. Memories.

Our Heart and Future

*W*e Ojibwe tend to be sentimental about our children, who are the heart and future of the people. Greatly loved as they are, their existence has such importance to not only their families but all Anishinaabeg that they will not know until they are adults themselves just how much they mean to us and the many reasons why.

Throughout history since the time of impact, Ojibwe families have experienced the loss of land and the lifestyles our ancestors lived on that land base. We have experienced the endeavors and experiments, some well-intended (I remind myself of this but then remember the old saying about the good intentions and the road to hell) and some not, of missionaries, boarding schools, homesteaders, land speculators; we have experienced the constant presence and pervasive intrusions of federal Indian policies. Survival of the family has been a struggle; today we continue to deal with the complexities of history that persist in our lives today.

How did a loss of land and relocation to reservation lands affect family life? Before reservations, Ojibwe extended families lived on a land base that was large enough to support a lifestyle based on seasonal sustenance: spring maple sugaring camps, summer fishing, cultivation and gathering, fall wild rice harvest camps, winter hunting and trapping camps. During the warmer seasons families prepared and saved for the cold winter months, and everyone in the family had a job and role in the process. Every person was created with a job to do, everyone was born with the ability to contribute to the group and the obligation to do so. In extended Ojibwe families, education began very early in life, accomplished by way of the oral tradition as well as experiential learning: children learned from their elders the satisfaction of helping family and community. In learning the creativity and skills of survival they also learned problem-solving, how the world works, and how to work with others. In listening to their elders they learned the history of their people, the traditions and teachings, and Mino-bimaadiziwin, the good ways to live. They learned that one day they themselves would become elders and teachers.

Here in Onigamiising and in the entire Arrowhead region this lifestyle changed greatly after the 1854 Treaty, which established the reservations of Bois Forte, Grand Portage, and Fond du Lac. The effect on the traditional lifestyle was immediate and severe. The government attempted to alleviate this with food supplies that held off starvation but created physical difficulties such as malnutrition and digestive problems for a people not used to flour, sugar, and dairy products. Physically confined and growing less healthy every day, families and communities struggled to survive. To thrive, or even to maintain, was nearly impossible.

The Treaty era ended in 1871 and was followed by the Indian boarding school era, which lasted from 1879 to 1934. During that time Indian children were removed from their families and sent away for formal schooling that was based on a federal policy of assimilation. I believe that this policy had devastating and far-reaching effects on American Indian families that continue today. For several generations of American Indian families the loss and absence of children became the norm. Extended family relationships were injured and broken, some permanently. The time-honored ways of teaching and learning were interrupted, for some families never to be continued. The privilege and blessing of raising children were cruelly denied, which hurt tribes and communities far beyond the family unit.

The heart's blood of a nation is its families, and the future of a nation is its children. In the years since the Indian boarding school era, and the policies and programs of the Termination era that followed, we have endeavored to retain some of what we lost and to maintain what we have. We remember what our grandparents and all who came before us endured, and we try to live the good lives they would want us to, honoring what is important, Bimaadiziiwin, which is the living of a good life. We are sentimental about our children, as our elders were about us. As parents and grandparents ourselves now, we at last understand why.

Summer Is Coming
to Onigamiising

*a*fter an unusually late spring a couple of years ago, we Onigamiising-ininiwag (people of the place of the small portage) became pretty excited at the signs of summer that were suddenly everywhere. It was near the end of May that I noticed that the remnants of Tim's nemesis, the big snowbank at the edge of the yard, had disappeared.

"Well, will you look at that!" I said. "That big pile of snow was just here, and now it's gone! When did this happen?"

He told me that the afternoon before he had chopped it with a shovel into pieces that would be small enough to melt in the sun. Walking across the yard to talk to our neighbor Kathy, I noticed tiny bits of greenery sprouting through the last fall's dried grass and leaves. "Summer's coming!" we said to each other, cheery about the possibilities of lush green lawns and Kathy's flowers.

As summertime nears, warmer weather and longer daylight hours, combined with the end of the school year, make for some happy and excited children, too. Listening to my granddaughters chatter about their end-of-the-school-year concerts, field trips, and classroom parties, I remembered how it felt to be that age, when in late May the summer ahead looked so long that we could hardly imagine the end and school starting again. And deliciously empty, each day just waiting to be filled with whatever we felt like doing.

My sisters, girlfriends, and I had a lot of fun in those days. We might not have had anything particular in mind, but at the beginning of summer we knew that the possibilities were the plans. Most mornings we slept as late as 8 or 9 a.m. and then usually helped with some chores around the house before we got going to the real business of summer, whatever that might turn out to be. We walked a lot, I remember: to each other's houses (where our mothers suggested that we go outside and get some sun!), to the library, and around about the neighborhood.

We babysat and often took some little child along on our adventures. If we had money, we took the city bus downtown and walked to the record store (where we flipped through 45s that I don't think we ever bought), to Woolworth's, and to the big department stores for window shopping. We chipped in for a jar of Dippity-do and used it to set each other's hair (and sometimes our little sisters') in huge pink plastic rollers. We cut paper dolls out of catalogs and created complicated, imaginary games for them on the front porch. After supper, we played ball in the field back of the house with other neighbor kids and our dad.

As my granddaughters talked and laughed about the exciting possibilities that the long days and weeks of the coming summer might hold, I thought that they sounded very much like my friends and I did at that age. Summers are more structured now than they used to be, and many children have full schedules of activities, lessons, sports, and playdates. I wondered what the granddaughters' summer would hold. Would every minute be planned out for them and scheduled? I wondered; might they have some time to enjoy summer days of unplanned and endless possibilities?

"Do you have some big plans for this summer?" I asked.

They looked at each other, thinking about the end of the school year and the prospect of those long days of summer, some that would be spent on planned activities and lessons and some, no doubt, waiting to be filled up with whatever they thought up next. And they smiled.

"Lunch," said one.

"Swimming," said another.

"Practice dancing," said the third.

And from the fourth, "I think I'll sleep late every day."

I think they might have almost as much fun as Tim did, chopping up the last of that snowbank.

Niibin

Summer

Chickens, Eggs, and Stories

One of my Facebook friends recently shared pictures of some of his chickens, the flock grown to ten in number, enjoying fresh air in their shaded little fenced-in yard attached to the coop. These city gals are, perhaps, distant cousins to my brother's chickens who live a more countrified life out midway between Duluth and Esko. They are, like almost all chickens in North America, descendants of immigrants.

Although game fowl has long been part of the traditional Ojibwe diet, domesticated chickens were brought to this part of America by missionaries and settlers. (Flocks of chickens were brought to the southwest by the Spaniards earlier, around the year 1500, and there is some historical evidence of chickens having been brought to South America by Polynesians even before that.) Chickens survived ocean voyages fairly well; they are small and easy to take care of; they produce eggs and more chickens, of course. In the more rural American economy of not so many years ago, just about every farm had chickens, and so did many city or town households, including here in Onigamiising.

Household chicken flocks are no longer common, but the number of people wanting to raise their own chickens has increased in recent years. My Facebook friend is one of these, as is my brother's family. The Esko-Onigamiising chickens were my sister-in-law Sarah's idea: she had been raised in a farming community and was used to having chickens around. When we visited to see the chickens, my brother Denny, who was NOT raised in a farming community, cautioned us, "Stay away from the rooster. He's mean." Denny is a former champion boxer and a pretty courageous guy, but did I see fear in his eyes? "Do you want to pet one? Wait here, I'll get one," said Sarah, who walked confidently into the fenced yard and picked up a chicken. My grandchildren cooed and stroked its beautifully iridescent feathers. When we left, Sarah gave us a carton filled with eggs of varying sizes and colors. "You'll like these; they are way better than the ones you buy in the store," she said with pride. She was right.

Urban chickens were not something seen every day when I was a girl, but I remember we often knew someone with a coop. My grandpa raised chickens right in town, in a very well-crafted coop with a high, shingled roof and a yard with both concrete and grass surfaces outside. The rooster and Grandpa were buddies; they even sometimes played tug-of-war with an old hat.

There was an elderly lady in the West End who didn't

always keep her chickens in her yard, which the neighbors found annoying. Friends across the road from our house in Kenwood became accidental chicken farmers when the cute little baby chicks they gave their kids for Easter grew up: their kind-hearted dad built a pen and a shed, and the LeGarde and Hanson kids had such fun playing with those pet chickens! And down the street from my family's house on Springvale Road a woman kept what was surely the neatest and cutest coop and henhouse in town, with chickens so groomed-looking that they could have been on a movie set.

The Ojibwe word for chicken is *baKAA-aKWAA* or *baKWAA-aKWENH*, the name/word for them that caught on when they and the immigrants who brought them arrived in Ojibwe country.

The old Ojibwe tell us that in days long ago the people and animals, including the birds, could speak to one another and understand. Perhaps the chicken arrived in Ojibwe country near the end of those days. Did an indigenous bird, perhaps a partridge, greet them when they arrived and ask, as is polite among the Anishinaabe people and our friends, "So . . . where are you from, and who is your family?" "Bukbuk cluk baKAA-aKWAA," answered the new bird. "Aaah, did you hear that? Let us be sure to welcome these newcomers and to courteously and considerately call them by the name they have spoken," said the partridge to the Ojibweg.

A true story? Maagizhaa (maybe); gayay maagizhaa nindikid (and maybe I am kidding).

Gii gawaabimin, until next time.

The Summer of
Our Favorite Toy

*L*ike many other families of the '50s and '60s the Le-
Gardes got a lot of use out of a baby buggy that was
traded back and forth between relatives. Ours was of
two-toned blue vinyl-coated canvas and the size of a
large bassinet. It could be removed from its collapsible
aluminum frame and used as a portable crib or in the
backseat of the car. The hood folded back; a compart-
ment under the mattress was handy for storing extra
diapers, bottles, and baby food. (Buggies had been
around for decades; my grandmother told my mother
that she had stashed doughnuts in hers when my dad
was a baby.) As the buggy was pushed down the street,
the wheels made a satisfying little click-click-click, and
the springs ever-so-gently jiggled and soothed the baby
during the ride.

Though they were bulky and heavy by today's standards, buggies made life more convenient in times

when few households had more than one car. Mothers could load several small children into the buggy and walk to the store, to visit friends, to school conferences. I have seen mothers actually hold a baby in one arm while folding the buggy, then carry everything onto a city bus!

Baby buggies were sturdy enough to last for quite a while, but they did eventually wear out: when the vinyl frayed and the springs began to sag and squeak, our dad took ours apart and put it in the trash. We kids weren't especially interested in a tired-out old buggy body, but when we saw the folded-down frame, so compact over those spoked wheels and egg-shaped sets of springs that looked like Christmas ornaments, our reaction felt like the excitement of Christmas morning. "Can we have this to play with?"

Our mom left the buggy body in the trash but let us haul the frame away from the garbage, and for the next several weeks the LeGarde kids had one of the coolest toys in the neighborhood.

Folded down, the baby buggy frame was a rectangle of several layers of aluminum rods spring-suspended over four wheels. It made a great go-cart: the buggy handle, which was covered by a ribbed rubber tube the width of the cart, became the place where a child flopped belly-down and suspended over the frame would hang on, chin above the handle and a fist on either side of the chin. Our driveway, unpaved and not too steep, was a short and thrilling ride of bumps with a turn at the bottom that, missed or not, ended the ride in the backyard, in grass.

Our mom didn't allow the little kids to ride, and she told us big kids to be careful. Were we? We pinched our fingers some, never enough to cry or go into the house. The wheelbase was broad enough that we didn't wipe out; however, thinking back I now wonder how it was that we didn't lose any teeth.

After a few weeks of being left outside, the buggy frame began to rust, which left orange stripes on our knees and palms. One morning when we went to the backyard (Mom made us keep it in back because of the way it looked), the buggy frame was gone! We were horrified at the thought of its being stolen but then found it next to the garbage cans. We rescued it, thank goodness, and brought it to the back door to tell our mother about the terrible mistake that had almost been made, and how lucky we were!

She started to laugh, and we heard her later in the morning telling our Aunt Peggy about it over the phone, laughing all over again.

A couple of weeks later the buggy frame disappeared again, this time for good, but since it was getting close to the end of summer, we were distracted by our thoughts of new shoes and who our teachers would be. And so we left behind one of the great times we LeGardes had as kids and went on to the many others ahead of us.

Weeds and Wildflowers

*W*alking through the mall a few weeks before school started I could see that business was really picking up in the shoe store. A young woman knelt on the floor in front of a little girl. "Wiggle your big toe," she said as she gently pressed her thumb over the vamp of a pair of tennies. "Where *is* your toe?" she asked, more to herself than the child.

"Would you like me to measure her feet?" asked the salesman.

As the little girl stepped onto the metal sizer, her mother asked, "Can we try a half-size bigger than that? She's been growing so fast this summer, and I want these to still fit her by the time they wear out."

It can be a little tricky, finding that size of shoe that leaves some room to grow but not so much that the child risks tripping.

Children do grow fast. As one of the grandmothers

in our extended family used to say when she saw (any of) us, "You're growin' like a weed!" There was delight in her voice, and I beamed and stood a little taller, picturing myself as a bright yellow blossom on a leafy green, leggy stalk that nodded brightly in the sunlight, growing as she spoke.

Children do grow like weeds. Or wildflowers.

Driving home from the mall my husband pointed out a bank of purple flowers at the side of the road. Did I know what they were? he asked. Were they weeds or wildflowers? We decided that for us they were wildflowers.

I am sure that there must be horticultural categories that define and separate wildflowers from weeds, but I think that circumstances and worldviews regularly blur the lines between the two. Dandelions picked from the yard by a four-year-old and presented in a stem-stained fisted bouquet to an auntie are surely wildflowers. Dug out of the yard on a sweaty afternoon just before their lovely gossamer fairylike seeds blow across the neighborhood and take root in other people's grass, I still think they look more like wildflowers than weeds.

Children grow like wildflowers and they grow like weeds. Later that same day I went to my sister's house for cake and ice cream; it was her birthday celebration, and among the guests were her children and grandchildren. "Ben, you have really grown this summer; you are almost as tall as your mother!" I said to one of the boys. He beamed and stood taller still, or perhaps he was growing even as I spoke. Next time I see him I will try to remember to tell him that he is growing "like a weed."

The little girl in the shoe store wiggled her big toe in a pair of tennies one entire size larger than the pair that her mother told the salesman she had bought at just the beginning of summer. The smile on her pink wild-flower face was rosy with pride and pleasure that she had outgrown her shoes. "Can you walk for us, so that we can see how they fit?" asked the salesman. "They have room to grow in the toe and don't slip at the heels at all; I think they're a good fit," he remarked.

At the end of the aisle as the little girl turned and headed back toward her mother, she stopped to stare at a display of ladies' high heels of faux leopard skin. "Now, *that's* a pair of shoes," she was probably thinking. I remember my own little girls doing something similar, with a pair of silver sandals (wasn't that just last week? I guess not), and a few winters ago, my granddaughter Mary, who is a pink peony, staring with such quiet longing at a ladies' size 4 party dress, short navy chiffon with a silver-sequined top, on a clearance rack, that I said, "Should we buy this dress?" and did. It was about the best $5 I ever spent. And what use might a nine-year-old girl have for a cocktail dress with a stretchy sequin top? Hours and hours of fun and thought while imagining the future.

They do grow like weeds and wildflowers.

Terry and Rachel Enter the Landscape of Nanaboozhoo

On hot summer afternoons when the air at the University of Minnesota Duluth gets very warm and steamy, I sometimes take a break to visit the nearby Tweed Museum of Art. The Tweed's temperature and humidity are kept within the optimal range for the well-being of its collections; visitors can enjoy the art in comfort, too.

The Tweed is one of my favorite places. It is open every day except Monday, and there is no admission charge (they do accept donations). The building is named for George and Alice Tweed, whose collections of nineteenth and early twentieth century European and American paintings became the foundation for the University of Minnesota's art museum. Mrs. Tweed donated the Tweed Gallery building to UMD in honor of her husband. The art collections and the building, which opened in 1959, have grown over the years; today most of the Tweed collections, as well as art exhibits from other collections, are displayed on a rotating basis.

In recent years the American Indian collections at the Tweed have expanded considerably, from both donations and purchases; the breadth of the collection is impressive in era as well as in representation from diverse tribes. In a single visit I can look at some very contemporary Native paintings as well as arts and crafts made a very long time ago. On the second floor a large glass walk-around case displays some of the Richard and Dorothy Rawlings Nelson eclectic collection that includes the work of many diverse tribes and artists. The items displayed are changed regularly: a visitor might see historical and modern cradleboards, clothing, bead and quill art, toys and tools, and household items. I like dolls, and there are always some in the case; especially appealing to me are dolls made and dressed more than a century ago.

On the first floor many are drawn to work by contemporary Native artists (Andrea Carlson, Jim Denomie, and Rabbett Before Horses are just a few of these). I will confess that I am by habit, and perhaps nature, a toucher of things, and so when viewing art I usually clasp my hands behind my back as I communicate with the paintings. I consider lives, experiences, and histories; I lean closer (with hands behind my back!) and wonder at the ability of brush strokes and layers of paint to tell individual and collective stories. Does the artist wonder what we will see while he or she works, do you think?

One summery afternoon two of my teenage grandchildren came along with me to UMD to help carry
some books to my office. While they were there they
helped out a little more by dusting, straightening, and
tidying the bookshelves. As they worked the temperature climbed; I could see that they were getting warm
and thirsty-looking. We took a short walk to a drinking
fountain and then over to the Tweed.

Terry and Rachel admired the Potlatch Mountie
paintings, the clean lines and power of African sculp-
ture, the faces and groupings in a student photography
exhibit. They circled the glass case in order to view
the Nelson collection from all sides. Downstairs they
walked the length of the Tweed to see the Rabbett
Before Horses creation stories paintings, drawn to the
larger-than-life *Searching for Nokomis* of the deep-blue-
shadowed forest, sky, and water, and the mysterious is-
lands on the horizon. I followed, noticing that one of
Terry's shoelaces was undone, and I opened my mouth
to say, "Tie your shoe," but as he approached the painting he looked so engrossed that I didn't want to inter-
rupt. Their backs to me, I watched them take it in,
and they too became a piece of the art: a seventh-grade
boy in baggy jeans, T-shirt, and sneakers, and a graceful
long-haired teenage girl, framed by the dreamlike azure
blue tones of the sacred story interpretation.

"I know this," Terry said to Rachel in his shy voice.
"It's Nanaboozhoo . . . see? There he is, and there's the
animals, and there's the turtle."

"Why does he have rabbit ears?" Rachel asked.

As my grandson explained quietly, I stepped back for an even better look at this piece of Ojibwe art, *Terry and Rachel with Nanaboozhoo,* which is now housed with the rest of my collection, intangibly and indelibly, in my memory and heart.

The Stone Tomahawk

It was the shiny paint job that drew my eye to the floor, where it lay under a wooden end table that displayed several imported resin figurines of scowling Indian chiefs and yearningly pensive maidens. The stone tomahawk, like the fanciful figures of imaginary Indians, had been bypassed by seekers of genuine Indian art and artifacts, who likely thought it a Boy Scout craft project.

And it was the shiny paint job that caused me to kneel there, on the floor of the old warehouse converted to specialty and antique shops, for a closer look. Attached to the handle, a ten- to twelve-inch length cut from a poplar branch, was an irregular oval rock the size of my fist, painted with red and yellow geometrical designs, secured to the handle by a length of basswood fiber wrapped back and forth around the rock and handle in a figure eight. The entire piece had been shellacked; except for a little dust and that the wrap had become dried out and somewhat loose, it looked tourist-shop new. And although I had not seen it before, familiar to me.

I have many times heard my father and my uncles talk about the tomahawks and war clubs they used to make to sell as souvenirs at their family's Indian tourist stand, decades ago, on the Grand Portage reservation; we have a photograph of my grandmother and aunt, assembling and painting tomahawks at their kitchen table in Duluth, and packing them in a cardboard box to bring up to the reservation. Could this possibly be one of the pieces that they made for tourist trade, I wondered, and should I bring my dad downtown to see it? My father was an Ojibwe elder; he was born in 1929, just months after the Merriam Report was released and Indian children began to return to their families from the federal boarding schools that most Indian children were sent to between 1879 and 1934. He was born five years before the Indian Reorganization Act and the establishment of the tribal governments that we know today. He married and raised his children during the federal government's Termination Era policies, those decades between 1950 and 1980 during which tribal sovereignty (and our birthright, and our identity as Indian people) was under siege. He witnessed decades of changing federal Indian policies and governmental attempts to solve the "Indian problem" that our ancestors somehow inadvertently created for majority America merely by existing. During those decades our very large extended family has survived, and often thrived. *Should*

I bring him to the antique mall? Indian family histories are collective and complex, walked by ghosts of past, present, and future bearing forged chains that can rattle and clank painfully when shaken, sometimes by what might appear outside of Indian Country to be the most innocuous of questions. *Should I ask if he would like to see the stone tomahawk?*

I thought about it for a couple of days, then stopped by for coffee and asked.

He wanted to go.

At the antique mall he lifted the stone tomahawk from the floor with two hands and looked down at it for a good minute without saying anything while I waited, touching and peering at the resin chiefs and princesses, a dried and cracking birchbark basket, the grimy gilt frame around a print of *The End of the Trail*.

I cleared my throat. "The wrap is a little loose," I said.

"That's easy to fix; a little glue would fix it, right underneath; see, right there." He looked down again, past the rock, poplar handle, paint, shellac, and spruce root, through more than half a century. I looked too, wishing that I could see what he saw.

"I'm going to buy this," he said.

An Impromptu Reunion

t hat late summer morning my mother called. "This is your Great White Mother speaking. What are you up to?"

"Nothing much; going to go into work, get things ready for fall classes."

"Well, would you want to come by for some coffee? Barney's here, and Jean and the cousins, too!"

My dad's brother, my Uncle Barney, had stopped by with his wife and some of their kids on their way back from the Rendezvous Days powwow at Grand Portage, but this was not an ordinary "stopping by." Barney and Jean were going to be dropped off in Washington State, where they lived, by their daughter Bernie and her husband, Rick, who would then head to their home in Colorado. Rick's van would travel for awhile in company with a Harley and a truck: the Harley ridden by Barney's son Ray, who would stay in North Dakota, and the truck driven by Barney's other daughter, Marie, and her boyfriend, who would proceed to their home in Arizona after leaving Bernie and Rick in Colorado. Whew!

By the time I arrived at my mother and dad's, there were quite a few vehicles in the driveway and in front of the house, as well as several people, including my niece Becky, who lives across the street and her little kids, walking into the yard. Everybody wanted to visit, and what a beautiful summer day it was for an impromptu family reunion.

My sister Nancy had made a trip to Johnson's Bakery, in the West End, to pick up some rolls and donuts (I always think Johnson's pastries look like jewels in those white bakery boxes), and my mother had set out some plates of homemade cookies she always seems to have ready. Everything looked very pretty, with patterned napkins and an assortment of fruit juices as well as fresh coffee, though the morning was a little warm for hot drinks.

We had a wonderful visit. Barney and Jean and the cousins told us about the powwow: how the weather was, who they had seen, what changes there had been since their last trip up north. They had run into rain on the way to Grand Portage, and Ray got really wet. We cousins watched the little kids run around the yard and play, just as we had when we were that age. Just as Barney and my dad did when they were that age. We watched, commenting on which little one looked like that cousin when he was little, just as those same kids will themselves, one day.

We laughed a lot, told each other how good we look. My sisters and I agreed that Marie's boyfriend, who we were meeting for the first time, is a great guy, so courteous and nice to everyone. My dad said several times to me as an aside, "Isn't it great to have Barney and everybody here? It sure is nice to see them." A year later, when Alzheimer's had taken a grip on his brain though never clawed its way into his spirit, I remembered how happy he was that day, and how thankful to see his brother.

Susie took some pictures of Barney and my dad, another in a long line of photos of the seven brothers, never all in the same picture, from the time that my dad was a baby and Barney a small boy, just before Barney left home and their mother for the Red Lake Indian boarding school far away in northwestern Minnesota. In every single picture I have ever seen of my dad and Barney together they have looked happy. Barney and Jerry had large families, a lot of kids and many grandchildren. They considered themselves to be lucky, and they were: who can be luckier than men who appreciate the good things that life has given them?

When it was time for the relatives to leave we all kept smiling; although it would be awhile before we saw each other again, and for some this would be the last time we all said, "Next year, next year! Gii gawaabimin next year at powwow time!"

In Ojibwe language there is no word for good-bye. We say in English, "See ya," or "See you soon." The lovely word that is used in parting, gii gawaabimin, translates literally in English to "You will be seen again by me," but when we say it there is also a deeper, spiritual meaning. We are taking leave of one another, but we will see each other again; and if we should not, then we will see each other some other time, perhaps in the next life.

It is a sweet and at times heartbreakingly beautiful way to end a visit while looking forward to the next.

Shii-waaboo

On hot summer afternoons many of us quench our thirst and cool off with a soft drink. That carbonated deliciousness goes down easily, soothing the mouth and throat; the cola, lemon-lime, and root beer flavors please the palate, and our thirst is satisfied. But only temporarily: within ten minutes the ingredients in soda pop can actually make us feel thirstier than before we drank it.

There are a few Ojibwe words for pop. For me, the easiest one is the simple *shii-waaboo,* sweet water. I believe that this word was used generically for quite some time to describe a beverage of cool water that has been enhanced with flavor and sweetness; however, for at least the past half-century it has come to mean carbonated soda pop.

We Anishinaabeg of the early twenty-first century live our everyday lives in ways that are very different

from our ancestors. Our clothing and food come from
stores; we travel and communicate very quickly by car
and cell phone; we regularly eat away from home, at
restaurants or food courts. How convenient it is to stop
at a fast-food counter and order a meal that comes on a
tray, how easy and fun, actually, to fill a large cup with
whichever pop you choose that gushes and sprays from
the dispenser.

Where might we find Mino-bimaadiziwin, the
Good Life, in the midst of chicken nuggets, fries, a text
message, and a large pop that just slid around on the tray
and spilled sticky liquid on the floor? In our existence
of contemporary choices, convenience, and complica-
tions, it is not always easy to maintain and continue
Anishinaabe knowledge and traditions.

And yet we do. Surely our ancestors had many tasks
to take care of every day that needed their attention and
concentration. The traditional Ojibwe seasonal lifestyle,
which involved moving several times during the year to
maple sugar, wild rice, and summer and winter hunting
and fishing camps, surely required extensive planning
and physical work. Every day was as new to them as
each new day is to us.

I believe that we live Mino-bimaadiziwin in ways
similar to those of our ancestors: in everyday lives that
are given to us by the Creator. The beginning of each
day is an unopened gift, and as the day goes by, we acknowledge that by doing our best to live the values that
have been passed down to us for generations: gratitude,
modesty, generosity, and a consideration for others and
the world around us. Living a good life is our gift back

to the Creator; our daily contributions, big and small (this would include mopping up spilled pop), continue the tradition of Mino-bimaadiziwin.

My own contribution today will be very small: I am thinking about raspberry tea, a longtime favorite Ojibwe beverage that long ago was served hot or cold. Today I will make a quart of raspberry tea, from the box of herbal teabags in my kitchen cupboard.

Traditionally, raspberry tea was made by steeping dried berries in hot water. Thinking about picking berries, drying, storing, and taking care to make sure the supply lasted until the next growing season reminds me of how labor-intensive our ancestors' lives were, and how close they lived to their food sources.

Here in Onigamiising at the beginning of the twenty-first century, I will boil the water in the teakettle, steep the tea to a light rosy pink, sweeten it with a little sugar, and keep it in a pitcher in the fridge. When my grandchildren stop by, I will add ice cubes to the pitcher and then serve them, in a twenty-first-century fashion, the same cool summer thirst quencher, shii-waaboo, that Ojibwe children drank generations ago. Onishishin.

Life Lessons from My Dad
and Jim Thorpe

*f*rom the front room window I watched several of our grandchildren playing in the yard, some climbing the tree in front of the house and the rest rounding up the plastic bat and looking in the grass for the practice balls. Although I couldn't hear them, I could see their conversation bounce around like a double play that tagged the two youngest children, who came into the house. When we were kids we used to do the same: send the youngest and most adorable to ask for cookies, or for ten more minutes outside before bedtime.

Because the adults were having coffee and talking, the grandchildren politely waited for us to pause and asked if Grandma would come outside and pitch for them. I put on my tennis shoes and went out to where I determined the pitcher's mound would be. A couple of the children are pretty heavy hitters. And some ticked a lot of balls. "Tick ball; no strike!" I called.

When we were kids we loved playing ball with our dad in the field behind the LeGarde house. He was a willing pitcher, and some of us were pretty good hitters and runners, too. We had a great time. Having a big family is a real advantage for baseball whether you're teaming up or, as we did, counting individual runs. It gives plenty of opportunity to try out positions, too. My brother Jerry was a competent catcher, and my sister Janet could throw. My own talents were very limited, but I was a fast chaser of groundballs in the outfield.

There have been a lot of athletes in our family as well as a love of sports, of not only the games but the philosophies and values in sports that can be applied to life. The building of physical and mental skills, clarities and complexities of thought, and a type of respect for self and others based on a developed philosophical, even spiritual, resiliency are all part of athletics. There are lessons to be learned through watching and playing sports.

Our dad sometimes talked of Jim Thorpe, the great all-around athlete who won gold medals for the pentathlon and decathlon in the 1912 Olympics. Jim Thorpe was one of our heroes: he was a Sac and Fox from Oklahoma who, as a Carlisle Indian School athlete, ran track, played football, baseball, and lacrosse, and won a national ballroom dance championship. Later he played professional football and baseball.

Jim Thorpe experienced many difficulties in his life: among these was the revoking of his Olympic medals (he had played semi-pro baseball briefly, during two summer breaks from school), which were eventually returned by the International Olympic Committee after his death. Thorpe had attended several Indian boarding schools from the time he was a little boy. At Carlisle he excelled in athletics and was part of the Carlisle Indians football team that won the famous Carlisle–Army game in 1912. When he talked about Jim Thorpe, our dad always mentioned the Olympic Committee's decision to revoke his medals, the greatness and versatility of Thorpe as an athlete, and the fact that "he could do anything; there was nothing he tried that he couldn't do."

The story of Jim Thorpe, of American Indian boarding schools, and of the student athletes who came through that system has affected several generations of American Indians as well as the entire country. A very readable and informative book about the topic is Sally Jenkins's *The Real All Americans: The Team That Changed a Game, a People, a Nation.* Through a recounting of the historic 1912 Carlisle–Army football game, Jenkins provides a good look at the athletics, journalism, historical events, and Indian and non-Indian relations of that time period; the effects of land loss, removal, and boarding school policies on Native people; and also how "real All Americans" affected sports, education, and life in America. The events leading up to the Army–Carlisle game, the game itself, and the lives of athletes are interwoven in this book.

As I threw underhanded pitches aimed towards where I anticipated my grandchildren would swing, I thought of the days the LeGarde kids played ball in the field in back of the house, and of our dad who was willing to spend that time with us after a long day of hard work. I remembered hearing him talk about Jim Thorpe and other heroes through the games we played and the stories we heard became part of us, too. And I called to the children as I remembered our dad, the everlasting pitcher, calling out, "Heavy hitter up! Move back!" and "Tick ball! That was close!"

Buckskin Ladies,
Ribbon Dress Girls

O ne of my favorite pictures is of my daughters taken
the summer when they were eight, six, and two. In
this snapshot they are holding hands and wearing their
ribbon dresses: Brenda in rose pink, Denise in green,
Abby in lavender. The dresses, made of floral-printed
calico, have open butterfly-style sleeves and ribbon
trim, and matching leggings. And because the dresses
look freshly ironed, the picture must have been taken
before we left for a powwow, not after we got back
home.

Although powwows are held year-round, summer is
usually thought of as the season for social powwows and
large gatherings. This goes back to days long ago when
travel, and access to food and shelter while traveling,
was easier during the summer.

Powwows carry on traditions that sustain us as Anishinaabe people. They are part of the continuity of

Mino-bimaadiziwin, the living of a good life. At each Grand Entry the sight of the dancers, drums, spectators, and the people who work so hard to make the pow-wow happen reminds each of us that we are a part of something much larger than ourselves.

During Grand Entry the bearers of the eagle staff and flags enter the circle first, then the male dancers. The Women's Traditional dancers lead all of the female dancers into the powwow circle. Traditional dancers have a distinct style that is understated, dignified, and quite graceful. Their steps reflect their demeanor, creating a slight sway to shawls, fringes, and the hemlines of their skirts. The other female dancers follow: jingle dress dancers, fancy shawl dancers, and little children. When all of the dancers have entered and the first song has finished, the powwow circle is complete.

Within the group of Women's Traditionals are ladies in buckskin dresses as well as ladies in cloth dresses, both solid colors and floral calico prints. The buckskin ladies dance at the head of the line. They are acknowledged with this honor for many reasons: one is that they are wearing clothing made of the same materials and in much the same way as that of our ancestors. The wearing of buckskin continues Ojibwe tradition and values that tie together hand, heart, and the world around us to the unseen world and the Great Spirit Creator.

Those who wear cloth dresses also demonstrate our history, culture, and spiritual ways. Their clothing tells a part of our story of adaptation and survival. Woven cloth came to this part of the world with the arrival of the European explorers and the fur trade, as did

thread, scissors, needles, ribbon, and trim. Trade goods
were integrated into Ojibwe life, embellishing clothing, household goods, and tools while saving time and
labor (the fur companies encouraged this extra time to
be used for trapping and processing pelts).

The addition of wool and cotton fabric, including
blankets, was a convenience and technological change
that Native people adapted to and in many ways made
our own. One example is the style of the Traditional
Dance dress made of wool fabric, with straps and a long-
sleeved jacket and ribbon striping trim. Buckskin dresses
of long ago were made of a single or double hide, with
minimal sewing (sinew was threaded through holes
punched in the hide), shoulder straps, and a sleeved
jacket for colder weather. Although they were sturdy,
the construction of buckskin dresses was labor-intensive
and took a lot of time. When pelts were traded to the
fur companies in exchange for blankets, ladies adapted
the same pattern of the buckskin to blankets. Many
blankets had stripes across the ends; the striped end of
the blanket, folded over the top of the dress, draped
gracefully onto the chest. They called the stripe the
"rainbow" of the dress, and we still do so today.

With the addition of trade cloth, particularly cotton
calico, which is lightweight and easier to work with
than buckskin or wool blankets, clothing construction
became faster and less labor-intensive. Clothing made
of machine-woven fabric may not have lasted as long
as buckskin and was not as sturdy, but it was easier and
faster to fit and sew. Both men and women wore calico
prints, and some women went into business for them-

selves, sewing shirts that they sold or traded to fur traders and voyageurs. (Some tribal communities expanded
their business to moccasins, pemmican, and buckskin
shirts and leggings.) At powwows today we still see
many men and women wearing printed, often floral,
calico as a part of their dance outfits.

In the photograph of my daughters as little girls, their
calico dresses look similar to the dresses of little girls
a century before that. However, times do change. It's
not unlikely that when we got back from the powwow
their dresses went right into the washing machine. On
the gentle or hand-wash cycle, because of the ribbons.

Aniin miinik ish tiktik? Berry Time!

*a*t the time of year that berries begin to ripen we especially appreciate the Creator's gift of these pretty and delicious little treats. I love the color and taste of berries; with each one that I eat, no matter what kind, I think, "This is my very favorite." When the strawberries ripen, I remember how they looked and tasted and smelled when we kids picked them in the field back of our house, years ago. They were warm from the sun, and so small and sweet and fragrant. When raspberries ripen, I remember when we picked them from the bushes in our grandfather's yard after supper, before the sun had gone back of the house across the street. Those raspberries looked like dark red rubies, smelled just a little like roses, and were the temperature of a warm summer evening.

Although summer is the season for fresh berries, we Anishinaabeg have enjoyed them year-round for many,

many generations. The Ancestors of long ago preserved them for the rest of the year by drying them for storage. Our grandparents dried berries, too, and their generation also had the technology to freeze and can them. These days we can freeze, dry, or can berries, and unlike generations before us, we have the convenience of buying fresh berries year-round at the grocery store, which means that even though they do cost more after summertime, we can enjoy berries long beyond our short northern ripening season.

Not long ago I made muffins with fresh blueberries, and the taste of berries and baking reminded me of the blueberry dumplings I haven't made for awhile. My own kids used to really like this, and I am going to share the recipe with you.

BLUEBERRIES AND DUMPLINGS

This recipe can be adjusted for the amount you want to make, for example, more or less blueberry sauce, more or fewer dumplings; however, the dumpling ingredients need to stay in proportion (for example, if you want double the dumplings, you will need to double all the sauce ingredients).

DUMPLINGS (make these first and let the dough sit while you make the blueberry sauce):
   1½ cups of flour
   3 tsp. baking powder
   ½ tsp. salt
   1½ cups of milk (you might need
      to add a little more milk)

Mix together the dry ingredients in a bowl. Gently add
the milk, mixing to make a dough that is nice and soft
(don't overmix because that makes the dough tough).
Let this sit while you make the sauce.

BLUEBERRY SAUCE

　1½ to 2 cups of blueberries, maybe
　　a little sugar if you like sweetening

Clean and rinse the blueberries, heat them in a saucepan
until almost a boil (you might need to add a little water).
Turn the heat down to simmer; watch and stir occasionally. Keep this on the stove burner.

　Spoon the dough by teaspoonfuls onto the blueberry
sauce and then cover. Let this cook, covered, for about
10 minutes (dumplings need steam in order to cook
properly, so don't lift the cover during that 10 minutes
unless you *just have* to). Lift the cover and check the
dumplings to see if they are cooked in the middle (I
poke them with the point of a steak knife to see how the
inside looks). When the dumplings are done, remove the
saucepan from the heat, take off the cover, and let it cool
about 15 minutes.

　This is ready to serve, and good as it is, or with a little
ice cream on top. If you like your dumplings to have
some sparkle and sweet flavor, you can sprinkle some
sugar on top just before you cover the saucepan, or a mix
of cinnamon and sugar. When berry season has passed,
you can use canned or frozen blueberries (thaw them
first), or even canned blueberry pie filling, though with
the pie filling you will have to check more often to make
sure the bottom doesn't scorch.

　Mino-pagwad: it tastes good, if I don't say so myself!

The Girl Cousins
Throw a Party

*t*he arrival of a baby is always a happy occasion in our extended family, and we looked forward to meeting the newest little one sometime in mid-August. My niece and her husband spiffed up the bedroom with some fresh paint, and their toddler-aged daughter moved into a bigger-girl bed. The crib was ready and waiting. All that was needed was for the baby to make his appearance sometime during the next month. And a party.

Some of the girl cousins decided to throw a tea party/luncheon/baby shower, with some help from their mothers and grandmothers. They had a great time preparing for the event: they planned mini peanut-butter-and-jelly sandwiches, pretty cupcakes, and other treats and invited their guests to wear "tea party clothes." Because the ages of these girls range from one to eighteen, and some get quite creative, it was very interesting and fun to see what *tea party clothes* meant to each guest!

The tea party was held at my house, and in the midst of the festivities I felt tremendous gratitude for the privilege of having children around. My grandmothers didn't have that privilege.

At some point during the years I was the ages of the girl cousins, I became aware that when my uncles and grandparents were children, they had not lived at home with their families. Instead, like many other American Indian children of those times, they had been sent away to Indian boarding schools and rarely saw their parents (and, in many cases, each other). I wondered then, from a child's perspective, how such a terrible thing could happen. As an adult, I learned about the history and mechanics of just how it did happen (although I still cannot really get a grasp of the reasoning). From an adult's perspective I try but cannot begin to imagine what it was like, the devastated strangeness of childless Native communities during those times.

Not that my relatives talked about devastation and trauma. Instead, when the subject came up, it was in bits and pieces: brief mention of working in the school laundry or kitchen; learning to mend clothing; a church group that visited the school with cookies for the students on Christmas Day; the disciplinarian who was cruel; the boys' prefect who treated them all right. And, especially, missing their mother.

Although this part of our history, as well as other bizarre and destructive Federal Indian policies to come in the later twentieth century, are not part of every-

day conversation, it is nevertheless an undertone running far, far below the surface of sending our children
off to school in the morning and rejoicing when they
come home at the end of the afternoon. The everyday routine of having children as part of the family and
community was disrupted for several generations of
American Indian people, and I believe this has given us
this particular appreciation for their presence.

The girl-cousin tea party/luncheon/baby shower was
something we hadn't tried before. Although the girls
planned and put the event together, behind the scenes
my daughters and I spent some time on the phone dis-
cussing who will bring what food. ("What time should
we get there?" and "How can we keep the sandwiches
fresh?" we asked each other.) Their daughters, my
granddaughters, worked on putting together party
games that the smaller girls could understand and enjoy.
("How will preschoolers understand the numbers on
the sides of the dice?" "We will use magic markers to
make each side a different color.") The favorite game
of the afternoon was the jelly bean game, invented by
Lindsay: come and take a jelly bean if you are wearing
socks; come take a jelly bean if you brushed your teeth
today; take one if you like kittens, etc. Each girl ended
up with a plastic cup of jelly beans!

By party time, the house was ready for the little girls
who would be our special guests: the table cloth ironed,
the fancy dishes set out, and the most comfy chair reserved for the most honored guest of all: my rosy,
blooming, expecting niece. Everyone ooh'd and aah'd
over the others' tea party outfits (mine was a new flow-

ered apron, with ruffles, and a pair of lace gloves), ate ridiculously dainty snacks, played party games for little prizes and favors, and admired the gifts for the baby.

The undercurrent of history ran far, far below the festivities, and we had a wonderful time. What luxury. Onishishin.

Tea with Scones and Stories

*O*ne year, in the middle of a series of unusual late-April blizzards, we LeGarde girls and our out-of-state cousins communicated through Facebook about their planned trip to Minnesota in August. They would be here for the Grand Portage powwow and for visits to relatives and places and memories from our own child-hoods as well as our fathers'. Would the snow be gone by then, we half-joked, and began to search the Internet for pictures of sunny, flowery gardens that we then posted on our Facebook pages. One that we especially liked was of a table set for an elegant, frilly outdoor tea party. Anticipating eventual warm summer weather (and trying to imagine the snowbanks gone and grass growing in the yard), we thought a tea party sounded like a fun occasion to look forward to.

Although our cousins relocated to out of state and have lived far away since the 1950s, our families have remained close in spirit, and we have a lot of fun when they get to Minnesota for a visit. We enjoy hearing each other's stories about our lives and what we are up to, and we especially like talking about the days when we were kids, and about our parents and grandparents. This preserving of history through the oral tradition comes from two directions: those who traveled to other places, and those who stayed in the area. It is really interesting how the stories have been passed from one generation to the next, which parts are emphasized in which families, and how the important and basic story line stays consistent and true.

We had a great time with everybody while they were here, but when tea party day arrived the guys considerately decided to go elsewhere and let the ladies have our own fun among ourselves (one of the girl cousins thought that the prospect of a ladies' tea party scared them off). And we did have fun: we set the table with a nice tablecloth and pretty dishes, with my sister Gail's pink-flowered pitcher and the aqua-and-pink dragon-patterned teapot that I got for Christmas one year. We used our best plates for scones, muffins, little sandwiches, and fancy rolls. The nicest decorations, though, were the smiling faces of the lady cousins and my mother all around the table. It really was a lovely afternoon.

After teatime we went outside to take some pictures, and then the guys arrived. Somebody commented on the weather, what a pretty day it was, just perfect (and I think they meant more than just the weather). And what a nice cool breeze. This made us think of fall and of school starting. The cousins thought they would take a drive to see the former Grant school, soon to re-open as the Myers–Wilkins Elementary School, which they had attended before they moved away. "Do you remember . . . ?" they asked each other—about their teachers, about the house they lived in that was near the school.

"See you next time," we said as we hugged or shook hands, and they got into the cars (it took two!). When will next time be? Perhaps next year; we would sure love that.

There is no Ojibwe word for good-bye. Instead, we say giigawaabimin, which means that we'll see each other again. If we don't, then we will some other time. And that is, as we Ojibwe say, pretty. Gaye onishishin.

The Gift That Grows
out of the Water

Manoomin, which translates into English language as "good seed," is the Ojibwe word for wild rice. Sometime in late summer to early autumn is ricing season, when manoomin has become ripe and ready for the harvest.

On reservations, the wild rice harvest is regulated by our tribal elders, band committees, and governments, who understand the importance of caring for and respecting the manoomin. Members of the band need a permit or license to rice; the beginning of the harvest is determined by the elders and other experienced ricers, who are knowledgeable about the wisest ways to harvest: when the rice stalks are of a color and size to be ready to yield the gift of manoomin to us.

Long ago, in the time before European impact, the Ojibwe lived out East, in the area that is today Maine to Newfoundland. When the Creator sent a vision to elders and dreamers that the time had come for the Ojibwe to move westward, our ancestors made the journey called the Great Migration to where we live today. The journey, which took many years and followed a route roughly along the Great Lakes area, was lengthy and difficult. This took fortitude and faith in the message of the vision. Part of that message was that the people would be provided for, that they would arrive at a place where food would miraculously grow out of the water. This was manoomin, the good seed.

The traditional way of harvesting wild rice is a labor of love that is physically demanding and exacting; every task involved in the harvest embodies the spirituality of the story and the sacredness of sustenance.

First, the rice is brought in from the lake. This takes two people, one to propel the canoe or rowboat through the rice stalks, and one to sit or kneel in the boat while knocking the ripe heads into a tarp, hide, or canvas in the boat with two wooden ricing sticks (these are about thirty inches long and made of a lightweight wood, probably cedar; it takes practice and strong arms and shoulders to do this).

The rice is then parched over a fire, in a large kettle. After that, the dried rice is placed in a clean skin, or a barrel, and danced or jigged upon by a person in clean moccasins made just for the purpose of cracking the hulls. The next step is winnowing. The rice is placed in a shallow birchbark winnowing basket and tossed up and down in the breeze (another task that takes strong arms and shoulders). The hulls and chaff blow away, leaving the finished rice.

If all of the steps are done properly, and if it is kept dry, manoomin keeps for a very long time. In the old days, stored dry, it was intended to last until the next year's harvest.

Technology has changed the way manoomin is processed as well as the number of people who still "finish" their rice in that way. Before the days of iron and copper kettles, manoomin was spread on deerskin hides to dry in the sun, which took much longer than parching over a fire in a kettle. With a seemingly endless demand for furs in Europe, many goods, including metal traps and tools, woven cloth, needles and thread, and iron and copper kettles, were traded to the Ojibwe for hides. These items shortened many of the tasks of daily living, including the time the people spent on processing manoomin (thus increasing the time they could spend on trapping and processing hides for the fur trade).

By the 1920s, in an economy that was becoming ever less barter-based and ever more money-based, technologies speeded up the processing of manoomin and the amount that could be finished in a shorter time. Machine-powered parchers could dry large quantities of wild rice very quickly; a person who owned a parcher could not only dry his own rice but could trade with or charge others to parch their rice. Some machine owners became middle men: they bought freshly harvested green rice right from the boats and processed it for sale to others who would distribute and sell it in stores.

In the 1960s, researchers at the University of Minnesota found how to domesticate wild rice, and for the Ojibwe, our very modest rice economy was severely impacted; it has taken decades to rebuild to what it is today. Machine-processed paddy rice (which is harder, blacker, and takes longer to cook) can be found in supermarkets and convenience stores at a lower cost than real wild rice. If you buy wild rice in a package, read the label: under Minnesota law, it will tell you if the rice is paddy (cultivated), and where it was processed.

Manoomin is a delicious, healthy, and versatile food that, when properly harvested and stored, has a long shelf life. Most important, the good seed is a gift from the Creator. Because of that, and because it is such an important part of Ojibwe history and culture, including our spirituality, we eat it respectfully, appreciatively, and prayerfully.

When We Cook Manoomin

*i*n many parts of the world, wild rice is a gourmet delicacy, which, because it is scarce and expensive, is served only on special occasions.

A few years ago some friends of ours had company visiting from the West Coast. Because we had such a good time meeting them and wanted to give them a nice gift, before they left town we gave them two pounds of Nett Lake rice to take back. They thanked us many times; later on those friends told us that they acted as though we had given them bags of gold.

That wasn't too far from the truth: manoomin, the good seed that is a gift of sustenance from the Creator, is a sacred food, its spiritual origin and purpose at least as precious as gold. Mewinzhaa, the Great Migration guided by the Creator, the Great Spirit who sent the vision of a miraculous food that would grow right out of the water, brought us to this place.

Manoomin, because of that spiritual beginning, is more than just food, more than physical sustenance. When we watch the stalks grow in summer, when we harvest, when we prepare and store manoomin, and when we cook and eat it, we do so in a thankful manner, remembering the great meaning of the good seed.

The wild rice that we gifted to our new friends was a variegated, medium-brown color, an indication that it had been harvested and processed in much the same way as it was hundreds of years ago: the heads loosened from the stalk, dried and cracked, winnowed, and then stored in a dry place where it would keep for a long time. (In my own experience, I have never seen rice that has been properly processed go bad.) That is the best kind of rice, and the kind that a person who "rices" and "finishes" in the old-fashioned way would end up with. Our new friends may or may not have known much about manoomin, but the appreciation they showed at receiving the gift did my heart good.

Here is how I cook manoomin: if it is for just two people, my husband, Tim, and myself, I scoop out a good-sized handful and pour it dry into a small saucepan. I cover it with room-temperature water and then use a sieve to rinse it, back and forth, six or seven times (traditionally finished rice can be rather dusty). I pick out any little sticks that might have gotten in during the processing. Next, I cover the rice with water and heat it to a boil, removing the saucepan from the burner when it starts to boil upwards. I skim any dust that boils to the top, turn the heat to low, and let it simmer, covered, for about ten minutes or so (checking a couple of times to make sure that it doesn't dry out), and then it is ready to eat by itself (my personal preference) or mixed up in a recipe. As far as that ten minutes of cooking time goes, that gets the rice to the point of staying firm (another of my personal preferences) and not mushy (to be avoided if at all possible—again, my personal preference!).

If I am not serving the manoomin in its plain glory, my usual way of fixing it is to cook enough rice for five to six servings and mix it gently with one can of cream of mushroom soup and some cut-up cooked chicken, meat, or fish. I bake it in a greased baking dish, covered, for about a half-hour or so, adding a little water if it looks like it needs it. Less is more with water; manoomin will keep on absorbing it the more you add (I have already said how I feel about mushy rice). The soup, which provides some cohesiveness and heat retention, is invisible by the time this is ready to eat; this simple "hotdish" looks like only manoomin mixed with meat.

And that is about as hotdishy as I get with manoomin: no onion, celery, or peppers, although some people do like to add them.

I also love manoomin mixed with some blueberries and, for a really good breakfast, a little milk or cream, raisins, nuts, craisins, cinnamon, and sugar.

Ninbakade, noongoom. Now I am hungry. Jiibaa-kwe daa ash wiisnini daa. Let's cook, and let's eat.

Gaye animay migwechiwendan daa. And let us pray our thankfulness.

Ready for Dinner

The letters *TBT* stand for "Throwback Thursday" in the parallel world that we know as Facebook. It has become the custom in Facebook culture to occasionally post a picture from the past on Thursdays, with a TBT designation before an explanation about the picture (for example, "TBT—my little niece Elsa with a bouquet of balloons, 2012" or "TBT: a picture from our wedding ten years ago today").

On a mid-August evening I decided to TBT a photo postcard that is more than a hundred years old. I had been out shopping that day and noticed some children and their mother looking at pencils, notebooks, and markers. I thought to myself, "Time to buy school supplies already?" Summer goes so quickly here in Onigamiising!

School was on my mind when I opened my Facebook page later that day, and I remembered the post-

card that I bought at an antique store. The postmark
(over a one-cent stamp) is from what is, in twenty-first-
century America, school-shopping season: that same
time of year, mid-August, but more than a century ago.

The message written in pencil is dated 8-23-14 and
says, "I am leaving this place for Marshall Minn. —Bert"
to a woman in New Philadelphia, Ohio. I cannot quite
make out her name, which looks like Mrs. John Fickes.
It was postmarked in Pipestone, and on the front of the
postcard is a picture of seventy-five to eighty boys and
girls in a crowded lineup across several buildings, the
largest one of brick with an arched entryway and two
cupolas. The jolly caption at the bottom reads "Ready
for Dinner, Indian School, Pipestone, Minn." There is
a slight distortion to the photograph, a waviness on one
side that creates an uncertainty to the balance of the line
of children; the buildings, however, have a solidity and
mass that overshadows the much smaller and harder-
to-see young individuals. Getting as close as I can to
the photograph I look into their faces, which appear
expressionless; as far as I can see there is not a single
smile among them.

I bought the postcard because my grandfather was
a student at the Pipestone Indian boarding school at
the time that Bert wrote to Mrs. Fickes (Fisher?). My
grandfather's name, Elias LeGarde, appears on Pipestone
enrollment lists sporadically until 1917. My grandfather,
who was born in 1900 (according to most of the annual
Indian Census records of that time), and his brother and
sisters attended several different boarding schools, most
of them in Minnesota. School records and correspon-

dence indicate that he was a chronic runaway who in the last Pipestone roster in which his name appeared was noted under the "Number of days of attendance" column simply as "deserter." In the national archives is a letter from his mother, my great-grandmother, written three years earlier to the Haskell Indian School in Lawrence, Kansas. In it she asked if the school would consider taking Elias, since his older sisters were students there and the children would like to be together at the same school. Since his name doesn't appear on any Haskell records that I have seen, and because in our family stories just the two girls went to what we called the "Indian college" in Haskell, I assume that the request was either denied or ignored.

Not long after I put the picture of the postcard on Facebook I heard from several people whose relatives had also attended the Pipestone Indian School. It was so kind of them to respond; the school operated for about sixty years, and I think that there must be many Pipestone descendants.

Pipestone was one of several hundred schools built for a particular purpose, which was to forcibly assimilate American Indian children into larger America. This was to be accomplished by the erasure of Native languages and cultures combined with instruction/preparation for jobs/vocations and some academic instruction. Assimilation, which was the key component of this educational system, necessitated the removal of children from their families and communities. The effects of this disturbing part of our history have been, of course, devastating and profound.

My grandfather was one of the children sent to Pipestone Indian School, as were the relatives of the descendants who contacted me through Facebook or e-mail.
Perhaps those other descendants, like me, looked very
closely at the photograph of the children lined up in
front of buildings that look so much more clear and
focused than the faces of the students "ready for dinner" (if they were, indeed, getting ready to eat; this was
a posed and planned photograph, after all), wondering
if they saw a resemblance to one of their own children
or grandchildren. In the face of a boy whose focus is on
something past the photographer and the camera I see a
resemblance to my grandson Jordan. Who might other
Pipestone descendants see?

It is not likely that we will ever know what Bert
was doing in Pipestone or why he was leaving (surely
that is a story in itself), and what was behind his taking the time to send a postcard to Mrs. Fickes (Fiches?
Frickes?). Something that I do know is that life is full
of patterns and symmetries, of mysteries and chances
seen and unseen that turn out to not be coincidental
at all. If I were to find that a descendant of one of the
students lined up "ready for dinner" at the Pipestone
Indian School was there comparing school supply prices
just ten feet away from me in the school supplies department at Shopko that mid-August afternoon, that
intersection of lives and histories would take my breath
away, and yet wouldn't surprise me at all.

Dagwaagin

Fall

Old Traditions
for a New School Year

*h*ere in Onigamiising, the place of the small portage, signs of dagwaagin, the fall season, begin to appear right around the time that the school year starts. My daughter told me that she was driving north to the Iron Range in early September of this year when she saw a small mountain ash tree just beginning to change color. The mountain ash in my backyard has stayed green so far, but the berries are heavy by September, and the branches are looking like they are beginning to tire.

When we see those early signs of dagwaagin, we know that it will soon be time for the children of Onigamiising to return to the world of pencils and crayons, teachers and books, classrooms and recess, to be schooled in preparation for the future, ours as well as theirs. We wish them success and happiness, and that they will use what they have learned to live good lives.

Mino-bimaadiziwin, the living of a good life, is at

the foundation of traditional Anishinaabe teaching and learning. A lifelong process, this requires commitment to learning through attentiveness, honest reflection, and hard work. We begin to learn before we are born, we learn something new each day that the Creator gives to us, we continue our journey in Mino-bimaadiziwin after we die and our existence moves to the spirit world.

Although tradition has come from our past, where it had its beginnings, it is with us today; we value and nurture those ways of our grandparents and do our best to educate our children so that those ways will continue. But in a world that looks so different from that of our ancestors, how can we maintain that traditional and timeless way of educating for the living of a good life?

Mewinzhaa, after the Great Migration a long time ago, the Anishinaabeg learned that in order to survive in the seasonal changes of this far north climate they had to rely on one another, to work in cooperation within their tribes and families. In meeting the challenges of living in the twenty-first century, those traditional teachings are as important as they have always been. Each person is created with the ability as well as the obligation to contribute something to the wellbeing of the group. It is the intent of the Creator that the people care for each other and the world around them. A respect for lifelong learning and education is integral to this important truth, which we instill in our children from a very young age through storytelling, example, and experiential learning. Like the Anishinaabeg of long ago we take pride in our children's self-reliance, their ability to make decisions, and their sense of responsibility to others. These qualities and life skills provide a solid foundation for a positive and fruitful education both in and outside of the classroom.

In the continuing tradition of Mino-bimaadiziwin, when we send our children to school it is our hearts' desire that they will grow and thrive, that their spirits will be nurtured as they learn, that they will succeed academically and socially. Here, then, are my own wishes for the children of Onigamiising as they begin the new school year: that they will enjoy learning and that they will be respectful of their teachers, their classmates, and themselves. That they will like school and have fun, that they will want to go there. That they will remember to do their homework on time, to keep their desks and classrooms tidy and clean, to behave courteously and considerately in the lunchroom and in the library, on the bus and on the playground. That they will not be too shy to ask for help, and that they will be kind and helpful to others. That they will know that they are loved and appreciated.

The Mystery of Indian Corn

As we travel through the seasons of our life's journey each year, we watch dagwaagin, the season of autumn, begin looking like summer and end looking like winter. As dagwaagin winds toward the fourth Thursday of November, so does Indian Corn season. Those decorative arrangements of colorful hard ears of corn that appear every year between Halloween and Thanksgiving disappear from front doors, mailbox stands, and teachers' desks and won't be seen again until next fall. Which is all right with me.

I don't know how Indian Corn season came to be. The Ojibwe people traditionally lived a lifestyle according to the seasons and called each cycle of the moon after the blessings provided by the Creator for that particular time. *Gashkadino Giizis,* the Freezing-Over Moon, is the term for November.

I have wondered about Indian Corn since I was in

the first grade, when Miss Johnson brought in a handful of little toy pumpkins and placed them on a table in front of the classroom next to three ears of shiny red and brown corn. Everything was all dried up and very hard and stiff-looking. The toy pumpkins were gourds, she told us, and the corn was Indian Corn.

Now, what in the world was Indian Corn? As an Indian child, should I have known? I wondered, hoping she wouldn't ask me about it in front of the class.

When we were kids, my brothers and sister and I loved corn on the cob, that sweet buttery summertime treat that made everyday meals a party and picnic meals a delight. Our dad loved popcorn, which I recall as a wintertime treat that our mother heated in a covered saucepan over the stove until it burst and ricocheted around in the pan with a sound like a hundred cap guns. We ate the popcorn salted and buttered, shared from a large yellow mixing bowl while we watched TV before bedtime.

But what in the world was Indian Corn? I wondered if Miss Johnson's corn was what popcorn looked like before it was scraped off the cob and placed in the Jolly Time bags that our mother bought at the grocery store for twenty-nine cents (from those bags came many bowls of popcorn). I wondered if uneaten cob corn turned red and brown and hardened as it aged.

Miss Johnson, thank goodness, didn't say anything more about Indian Corn but hung it on a nail next to the blackboard. When the classroom was decorated for Thanksgiving, I noticed that one of the red cardboard Indian men was wearing a bunch of Indian Corn, just like the bunch hanging from the nail, at the side of his breechcloth.

I pondered the mysteries of Indian Corn from time to time over the years when it made its decorative seasonal appearance in classrooms, on front doors, on yard light poles.

A few days before Thanksgiving last year I saw Indian Corn in another form, this at the grocery store, in a bag of that soft orange-yellow-white candy corn (another thing that we kids loved, come to think of it). This candy corn had a stripe of chocolate across the bottom, but I knew it was Indian Corn because that is what the big letters across the bag said: AMERICA'S #1 INDIAN CORN. I couldn't resist buying a bag to bring to the students who study, eat, and hang out in the Anishinaabe Club room at UMD. When I got home there was a letter from my Uncle Barney. He had enclosed a Thanksgiving cartoon of two Indians watching a ship sailing to shore. "Oh, come on; it's just one boatful. How much land can they need?" one man asked the other. In the morning I made a copy of the cartoon and brought it into the club room with the bag of AMERICA'S #1 INDIAN CORN. "Happy Migwech i Giizhigad from Linda and Uncle Barney. Enjoy this Indian Corn!" I wrote. The students laughed and snacked on the candy as they studied at their conference table.

To Speak Ojibwemowin

*h*ere in Onigamiising we are in the middle of the great Ojibwe Nation, which includes northern Minnesota and Wisconsin, upper Michigan, large areas of Canada just to the north of us, and some areas of North Dakota and Montana. Anishinaabeg have lived here for many, many generations. Up until my grandparents' generation, everyone spoke our native language, which is Ojibwemowin or Anishinaabemowin.

Although the learning and use of Ojibwemowin has grown somewhat in the past twenty years, not many of us today are fluent or even semifluent speakers. We would all like to be; we admire those who are. It is a beautiful language, and precious to us.

Ojibwe language was nearly destroyed during the Indian boarding school era. Between 1879 and 1934, official federal Indian policy was to assimilate Native people into larger America through formal schooling (this endeavor continued, under various policy names, until 1988; I don't believe, though, that it has ever stopped). During that period many children were removed from their homes and communities to live at schools where, as an integral part of their education, the speaking of their native languages was forbidden. English was the only language allowed at school. Consequences for speaking Ojibwemowin, as well as any other Indian languages, could at times be severe. Language is the foundation for communication and passing on knowledge, in every culture. For American Indian people, the loss of family, of cultural knowledge and worldview, of the simple comfort of communicating in one's own language was devastating.

In the heavily structured environment of the boarding schools, where federal assimilation policy was aggressively carried out, many lost the use of our languages. It only took a few generations: for example, although my grandparents both spoke Ojibwe, their children spoke less, their grandchildren and great-grandchildren less yet.

Although Ojibwemowin was all but destroyed, it did not die. There have always been people who knew how important it was to take care of the language, and to pass it on to others who would do the same. Here in Onigamiising, the Creator blessed us with the presence of Amelia LeGarde, one of our Elders who recently passed to the next world. A natural-born teacher, Amelia shared Ojibwemowin with many people, of all ages, Indian and non-Indian. Generous with her time and her knowledge, she taught our language both in the schools and community education, in formal and informal settings. Her teaching was truly a gift to us; we will remember what we learned and follow her example of sharing what we know with others. It is because of people like Amelia LeGarde that Ojibwemowin still exists. She has left to us a legacy beyond price.

Ojibwe language is taught at one of the elementary and one of the high schools here in Onigamiising. I have visited those classrooms occasionally, usually to tell them a story; for me it is always a treat. The students greet me in Ojibwemowin and treat me, their guest, with proper traditional etiquette, listening so sweetly as I tell them my favorite wintertime story (they love hearing about Nanaboozhoo's doings). What good changes there have been over the years: I could not have imagined such a thing when I was a girl in school.

I have been involved in Indian Education programs for nearly forty years and have seen educational trends, theories, and methods come and go; in Indian Country we continue to adapt and survive. If there is one constant for us, it is that we want our children to do well in school, and to always be proud of who they are. We want our children to know our history and culture; we are hopeful that they will have some knowledge of our language.

My oldest grandchild is now twenty-three. When he was a preschooler, we were visiting at my mother and dad's house with one of my uncles, an elderly man whose formal schooling had been at boarding school. My grandson was playing on the floor in back of Uncle Bob's chair, humming and singing to himself.

Uncle Bob asked, "Do you hear that? What's that he's singing? Can you catch the words?"

With some coaxing, Max came out from back of the chair and sang, bashfully, "Boozhoo, everybody, and wave at a Niijii!"—part of a song he had learned at Fond du Lac Head Start.

Bob nodded his head. He laughed softly, with pleasure. "You couldn't do that when we went to school, couldn't talk Indian; it wasn't allowed. These days they teach it right there, right in school." The elder held out his large hand toward Max, who placed his own small hand inside. "Keep it up; you're doing good," Bob said.

My grandson and my uncle shook hands, and although we were inside the house, I felt the warmth of the sun shining on us all.

Going Out to Eat

*t*o celebrate our daughter Denise's birthday we went out for lunch at the Pickwick, one of Duluth's historic old restaurants, and took along some granddaughters. It was clear to see in the girls' demeanors, in their very walks as they entered the building, that they felt quite grownup. Inside, they looked around the dining room at the furniture and museum-like décor as they sat at the table with the fancy carved legs, read the menu carefully, and ordered their own lunches. Like grownups.

Like many other birthday partiers at the Pickwick and other restaurants, we had brought a gift for the birthday girl, which she opened after we had finished eating. In honor of Denise's birthday the restaurant brought her a sundae with a candle on top. We sang "Happy Birthday" (very quietly, as this is a pleasantly and blessedly low-key restaurant); she made a wish and blew out the candle; she and the girls shared the ice cream.

I wonder if the girls will remember our little party, the photographs on the walls from earlier days in Duluth, the murals painted by Feodor von Luerzer, and the story that Tim and I told them about sitting on the curb across the street as nineteen-year-old spectators the time the restaurant had a big fire. Perhaps one day they will tell that story, as well as stories of their own lives, to their children and grandchildren.

Going out to eat is much more common now than it was when I was my granddaughters' ages, but I still feel the festivity of the occasion, whether it's a celebration at the Pickwick or a fast-food supper after work. It reminds me of the joy the LeGarde kids took when our parents brought home a bag of burgers and fries, not an everyday event in those days. What fun it was to be handed a hamburger wrapped in white paper and a good handful of deliciously soft and greasy French fries! I suppose our mother thought that not cooking that night was a treat, too!

An appreciation for food and the occasion of breaking bread with others is a part of Mino-bimaadiziwin, the living of a good life. We Ojibwe parents and grandparents (like parents and grandparents in countries and cultures all over the world) do our best to teach our children to be thankful: the values of modesty, gratitude, and generosity are intertwined and at the foundation of our traditional ways, which we teach to younger generations. Our teaching methods include modeling/ example, storytelling, hands-on experience, and of course, celebration. Education is lifelong, and what is learned is reinforced from time to time as we travel along life's pathway.

As I write this column I am reminded of one of those occasions, this one more than two decades ago when I was not yet a grandmother but would soon be.

Duluth's Director of Indian Education and I were accompanying an Ojibwe elder who was also a recently retired educator to St. Paul, where we would be attending a meeting about increasing the number of American Indian teachers in the state of Minnesota. We left Duluth very early in the morning and stopped along the way for coffee and breakfast. The elder, who was experiencing health and mobility issues, was using a wheelchair; she did so with good humor and a positive approach, although it must have been hard for a woman who had been a physically active leader in education and civil rights for decades. We were clumsy with the wheelchair, but she was patient and cheerful as we made our way from the parking lot to a fast-food restaurant. Inside, we got our food and brought it to the table, where we waited for the elder to begin. She opened her Styrofoam box and looked at the fast-food scrambled eggs, uniform-looking bacon strips, and little potato nuggets. She smiled, smelled the steam rising from the food, and said, "That looks luscious."

And I saw that it did, indeed, look luscious. She had seen and experienced what many people of her generation had—the difficulties and tragedies of twentieth-century Native America: boarding schools and the destruction of families; federal termination policies;

relocation and adoption programs; the disruption of her own schooling—too many indignities and broken dreams to count. Yet she stayed constant: she never stopped learning, working, and encouraging others, never stopped being a good, thankful Anishinaabe woman. And that morning she showed us that the fast-food breakfast was luscious and appreciated, and so was life.

How Much of an Indian Are You?

*l*ike every American Indian person I know, I have been asked, "How much Indian are you?" many times. Although I have tried to be ready for the question, and have even practiced in my mind how I would respond the next time, I never am.

"How much Indian are you?" People who would never, ever ask what I weigh or the amount of money I am paid to do my job slide it into a conversation, or as a question at the end of a presentation I have just made at their club, or during a diversity training session.

It is a personal question, and intrusive. I have wondered why people ask it.

My niece Julie tells me that people are well-meaning but curious, and that they don't think how the question might be taken. I have tried to keep her words in mind as I attempt to respond Ojibwe-style (courteously, indirectly, absolutely immovably), but it is not easy to do that.

The legal status of American Indian people is determined by many variables, including legal blood quantum, ancestral lineage, and the constitutions of the tribes, which are sovereign nations that determine membership requirements. The question of tribal enrollment status and legally documented and established blood quantum can be difficult to answer because of the complexities of history—compounded by the marriages and resulting descendants of individuals from diverse bands and tribes.

An accurate blood quantum can be difficult or impossible to ascertain. There are many reasons for this. One is that this information must be culled from Indian census records (American Indians used to have a separate, annual federal census taken) and land allotment records that are more than a century old. Not everyone's great-grandparents participated in the Indian census records, which were recorded at different intervals and with different information from the rest of America's census records. Blood quantum information handwritten by federal agents on these old census and allotment records often recorded different degrees of Indian blood (as well as names and spelling of names), even for siblings within the same family, and changed inexplicably from year to year.

Allotment records, which were intended to keep track of land parcels assigned to the individual members of the bands that had moved onto reservation lands, have the same inconsistencies. When acreage plots were allotted to those individuals, many lost their land, some misled and cheated by dishonest buyers or land speculators. In an attempt to put a stop to the avalanche of land passing from Indian ownership, the federal government declared full-blood (by officially recorded blood quantum) Indians legally incompetent to transact land sales contacts. Dishonest buyers then assisted many Indian people who, in trying to survive in the downward spiral of a changing and volatile economy, were desperate for cash money, in changing their blood quantums, on paper, to a lesser degree in order to finalize the sale. The resulting loss of land was devastating; the long-range effects of those reduced legal blood quantums continue to be experienced by their descendants today.

There are American Indian people who are not of a legal blood quantum, lineage, or date of birth that are needed to meet their tribe's requirements for application for enrollment. Some who were adopted out as children, especially from the 1940s through the 1980s, do not know where they are from, which tribe or band they might have connections to, or if they are actually Native or not. How many adopted or fostered people have I met during my lifetime who think that they might be Native, hope that by some miracle they might find this lineage, and when they cannot search by recorded census records, allotment records, or genealogical records, search by heart and spirit? I don't think I can begin to count.

The reply to the question "How much Indian are you?" is not an easy one. Not all Indians are enrolled in tribes. Of those who are, many have inaccurate, partial, or missing blood quantum records. Some are not enrolled but are direct descendants of enrollees. The legal relationships between Indian tribes and the federal and state governments have been a significant variable in the legal blood quantums of individuals—another one of those complexities of history. Some tribes and bands have federal recognition, some have state recognition only, and some are not legally recognized as sovereign bodies at all.

"How much Indian are you?" I am never ready for the question, although I have practiced a number of responses, to myself and with other Indian people (we laugh as we do this, but we know it isn't really funny). We have joked about silly responses we could have made, or could make the next time it is asked, and we have each of us lost our patience once or twice.

Why is this question asked of us, and what does it even mean?

I continue to practice my response; perhaps next time I will be ready.

"How much Indian are you?"

"Hey, did you watch the Twins last night?"

We Honor Native Veterans

*a*t the beginning of the twenty-first century there were nearly 200,000 living American Indian veterans of the United States armed forces. Here in Onigamiising as in all of Indian Country they are appreciated and honored in many ways. One of these is the opening ceremony of the powwow, the Grand Entry.

Grand Entry begins with the entrance of flag-bearing veterans, or people standing in for veterans, leading the dancers into the powwow circle. In this part of the country the flags are the eagle staff (sometimes called the Indian flag) and the American flag, joined by the Canadian flag and the POW/MIA flags. After all dancers have entered the circle, an elder prays the invocation, and then the veterans are honored with a special song. They dance the powwow circle; often, after they have completed one circle, we respectfully follow.

In Indian Country it is a big deal to be a veteran. A

student in one of the classes I teach noticed this when we were watching some filmed footage of a veterans' honoring dance. He asked what might be the reason for this; after all, he commented, American Indians were treated unfairly and badly so often throughout American history.

The reasons are rooted in Native worldview, the intertwined spiritual and cultural aspects of living a life of honor. American Indians have served in our country's military service with the highest percentage of any racial or ethnic group since records have been kept. During World War I, the U.S. Census recorded a Native population of less than 300,000 in the entire country, yet more than 12,000 served in the armed forces. During World War II, the Native population according to the federal census was approximately 350,000; of these, more than 44,000 served. More than 42,000 American Indians served during the Vietnam War; of these, 90 percent were volunteers. American Indian people, both men and women, have served in the Korean War, in Operation Desert Storm, in the Iraq War, in Afghanistan, and wherever they have been called to serve, in peacetime and war. They continue to serve today.

In the ways of Bimaadiziiwin, the living of the good life, the most highly respected people are those who serve and give of themselves to others. Those who have served, the veterans, and those who are currently in the armed forces follow the warrior tradition as living examples of selfless protectors of our people and land.

Our warriors in their journey through life truly learn what it means to combine strength, gentleness, pride, generosity, and gratitude—those qualities that create a warrior who will serve our land and people long after his or her time in the armed forces. We acknowledge this at many events and gatherings; the powwow is one of those occasions. We rise to stand when we hear the announcement that Grand Entry will begin. Standing, we watch our flags and our veterans pass first, before the other dancers. Standing, we silently and respectfully offer our thanks and good wishes. When the veterans' song begins, we watch our warriors as they complete one turn around the powwow circle; we wait for them to pass and then follow behind, dancing our prayers of appreciation and admiration for their service and sacrifices, freely given to us all with courage, humility, love, and grace.

"Welcome home," I think (and say aloud to some). "Welcome back to your land and your people. Migwech."

When Grandmother
Went to School

When I was growing up in the 1950s and 1960s, how and where my relatives had been schooled was rarely mentioned and never discussed. Instead, the schooling of American Indians prior to my generation was a topic to be avoided, a source of secrecy, sadness, and shame.

One of my uncles told me, when I was around six, that he had gone away from home to school. This was a different kind of school that he didn't like. My mother told me later that before I was born American Indian children were removed from their homes by the federal government and sent away to boarding schools. The story was a sad one, she said; it would make me cry if I knew about it, and I should be thankful for the life I had.

I spent my childhood and teen years protected from yet ever mindful of the sorrows of the past, trying to be a good student, trying to walk with dignity through the annual Indian unit at Thanksgiving time, trying to play the clown through thoughtless children's jokes about scalpings, trying to displace myself into another dimension when a boy imitated the staggering walk and slurred speech of an Indian man he saw going into a liquor store. I knew that I was luckier than my elders had been, and that my own school experience was a better one. I owed it to the past to appreciate and survive in the present; I owed it to the mysterious and wrenching experiences of my elders to be the best student I could.

I hung around with some nice girls, yet I remember a time we were standing in a circle in the hallway between classes (this was how groups of Lincoln Junior High girls socialized in the early 1960s at school) giggling and gossiping with the high drama of early teens, when one girl made a joke about Indians, and then another girl pointed at me and half-shouted, in the way of socializing girls of that age, "LeGardes are Indians!"

I smiled blandly, displacing myself into the dimension of no collective memory, no pain, only the silence of oblivion, but within seconds was brought back into the circling of menace.

She repeated herself. "LeGardes are Indians!" she shrieked, cackling, and the other girls laughed, too, all of them, as I was certain at the time, yet even in my memory of humiliation I clearly see my best friend, a girl who was so soft-spoken that this might have been the first time I ever heard her raise her voice.

She and I called one another "Shorty" and both wore cat's eye–shaped glasses, soon to go out of style, hers tortoise shell with rhinestones in the corners and mine pinkish tan with cameos on the corners. We were both quiet girls: the first time Shorty heard me raise my voice was when her neighbor's dog chased me onto the back porch; the only time I heard her raise hers was in that circle of girls.

"Shut up!" Shorty snapped. "Linda's hardly any Indian at all!" I took it as a gift of loyalty from a true-blue friend (my dad got a kick out of it when I told him).

Then the bell rang and the circle broke, scattered to classrooms on either side of the hall.

It wasn't until I was a mother of school-age children, and working in an Indian education program in the Hibbing Public Schools, up north on the Iron Range, that my Aunt Carol began to talk with me about the educational experiences of American Indians, and of our family in particular. Her story, told to me over a number of years, was a multigenerational one of boarding schools, homesickness, cruelty, racism, and, most of all, hopes and dreams broken and revived in the survival of an extended family.

From the beginning of her story, when my grandmother and Carol's mother were sent to a Catholic mission school in Canada along with some of their other sisters, to the heyday of boarding schools in the 1910s and 1920s, through the 1930s when the Indian Reorganization Act dismantled the Indian boarding school system and phased American Indian students into their local public schools (sweetening the deal with federal money), I experienced through Carol my family's role as participants in and witnesses to a vast experiment in the breaking of a culture through the education of its young. She would talk for an hour or so in the late evenings, until she had shared enough of our story to become sleepy and I had absorbed enough to become sleepless. Drained by the tale and honored by the burden, I would get up in the morning to get ready for working in Indian education. Bolstered I was, and at the same time daunted.

One morning, the feeling of my littlest girl's fine, rather wispy hair in my hands as I braided it, then crossed and tied the braids behind her soft, fragile ears brought to mind that she was the age my grandmother had been when she left home for boarding school, just five years old. My own precious five-year-old would be walked a few blocks to school by me, her mother, and we would see each other, and her nine- and ten-year-old sisters, that very afternoon after school and work.

In that moment I appreciated more fully the struggles and tenacity of my family as well as all Indian people, who in valuing family and culture made it possible for people like me to live with our own families and for our generation's children to experience an education that is in so many ways so different from that of our grandparents.

My little girl buttoned her sweater from the bottom up, the way her sisters had taught her. She picked up her snack bag and smiled. "Ready to go to school?" I asked.

Falling to Thanksgiving

*t*he big tree in our front yard is called a red maple, which does not mean that its leaves are red but that the circulatory system in its leaves is red, like a human being. She buds early in the spring, provides a lot of shade, and in the fall becomes unpredictable: some Novembers her leaves turn a deeper green that eventually darkens to brown and then drop from the tree slowly; some Octobers they suddenly turn a brilliant yellow that hovers like a large glowing cloud over the yard for a week and then, suddenly, falls to the ground in a heap.

Our grandchildren, when they were younger, enjoyed those golden October days very much! What a help they were, raking and shoveling and generally "cleaning up" the yard to a dome of yellow leaves that they jumped and rolled into, eventually creating a leaf-covered yard very much like the one they began to work on. We loved watching this from the front porch:

they took such pride in helping and such pleasure in active, laughing play.

Dagwaagin, the autumn season, begins like summer here in Onigamiising and ends like winter. In Ojibwe tradition, that season of change from summer to winter starts at the end of the wild rice harvest and lasts until the weather is cold and there is snow on the ground. Near the end of the dagwaagin season comes one of my favorite days of the year, Thanksgiving.

In the way of Bimaadiziiwin, the living of the good life, a good Ojibwe is thankful. The first Ojibwe word I learned, and the one my dad said is the most important one to know, is *migwech* (thank you). A nice Ojibwemowin translation for Thanksgiving Day might be Migwechiwendam-Egiizhigad, the day of thinking thankfully. I cannot help but think thankfully as I prepare (or, these days, help my daughters to prepare) and eat the Thanksgiving dinner feast.

We Ojibwe acknowledge special—and sometimes not so special but just for fun—occasions with a feast and expression of gratitude; our ancestors did this long ago, and we continue the tradition.

Thanksgiving Day was somewhat confusing when I was a little girl starting school. In first grade we learned about the "First Thanksgiving" that was a feast and expression of gratitude on the part of the Pilgrims and their friends, the Indians, at the end of a hard year and harvest. The Indians helped the Pilgrims out, we learned, and so were invited guests. In picture books, they emerged from the woods, walking through snow without hats, coats, or mittens.

I recall tracing our hands on paper, which we then colored in to look like feathered turkeys, and drawing geometric designs, squares, and triangles on strips of brown paper that the teacher stapled together at the ends and told us were Indian headbands. I recall wearing these as we sat in a circle on the floor with crossed legs, Indian-style, the teacher called it, watching as she set out on the chalk tray cardboard figures of a Pilgrim man in coat and knickers; a Pilgrim woman in a long gray dress who held the hand of a small girl dressed like her mother; two tomato-red men, nearly naked and with strangely pointed heads, who carried aloft large platters of food. These were the friendly Indians, the teacher explained.

From their appearance, they might have been from another planet. They didn't look like any Indian men I had ever seen: my dad and my uncles, whose skin deepened and sunburned to a beautiful red-gold tan with summer work, usually wore work clothes or blue jeans. I decided, without letting the teacher know, that the "First Thanksgiving" must have been mythical and had very little in common with our Thanksgiving Day at home.

There is another story I recall, this one from an evening near the end of dagwaagin, just a day or so before Thanksgiving. Our dad was home that evening with us kids, our mother a block away at church, where she had gone to Turkey Bingo with her friend Bernice. Every so often Dad went out to the sidewalk to watch for them walking home; we followed him in and out of the house like a row of little ducks. Eventually, our mom appeared under the streetlight, walking with fast and excited steps in the cold, clear night. Her hair bounced as she walked; when she saw us she called, "Look!" Her hazel eyes reflected the streetlight and shone with happiness and excitement. She might have opened her arms to us as she walked, but they were wrapped around a large and bulky burlap sack. "I won a turkey!"

The turkey, laid on the dining room table and unwrapped, still had its pinfeathers, and its feet. It was so big! Fascinated, I stroked a soft and wrinkled claw. How would we eat all this? I wondered.

Early Thanksgiving morning I heard my mother moving in the kitchen and got up to watch. She had clamped the meat grinder to the kitchen table and had just finishing grinding giblets, bread, and apples into her large mixing bowl, which she had set on a chair. Seated on the next chair she was squinting a little as she plucked pinfeathers from the turkey with a tweezers.

That done, she washed the bird and stuffed it (its feet had been removed by my dad!), placed it in the oven, and began to clean the cranberries. She tied one of her gathered-waist half-aprons around my neck and let me help.

When it was time to eat, our family and friends said our prayers of thanks and ate with enjoyment and gratitude for the turkey, the meal, for each other, for everything in life that the Creator gives to us.

Cradleboards and
Portable Babies

*W*hen my daughters were small babies, during the
1970s, I transported them around town in infant
seats, which were plastic baby carriers the size and
shape of a large shoebox open at one end and lined
with a padded plastic mat. The babies were secured by
a plastic belt, and the seat was propped up by a metal
wire underneath that could be adjusted to one of two
angles; the baby's legs dangled over the edge, which
was curved.

Infant seats were lightweight and easy to carry (much
easier than a baby bundled in blankets), and I think
comfortable for the babies, who seemed content. They
were popular shower gifts and inexpensive; mine cost
only a few dollars. Like most of the young mothers, in
the car I held the infant seat on my lap while my husband drove. The days I drove him to work and used the
car, I wrapped a blanket around the infant seat and seat-

belted my baby girl into the passenger side of the front seat of our '67 Ford Custom. She slept while I drove, looking comfortable and secure in her flimsy blue plastic shoebox.

My girls are adults now, with families of their own. When their babies were born, the hospital required that the infants be in a car seat for the ride home. Today's car seats are much larger and heavier than infant seats, and certainly much safer. But the purpose for both is the same: a secure and portable baby. They have this in common with their great-grandma, the cradleboard.

Although cradleboards differ somewhat from tribe to tribe, the basic design is a solid protective wooden frame, with padding for comfort and decoration that reflects tribal tradition.

The Ojibwe word for cradleboard is *tiikanaagan* (teeka-noggin). Ojibwe cradleboards have a lightweight padded-board backing with a shelf at the bottom for little feet, and a bentwood "roll bar" near the top, which protects the baby's head and face. In back is a carrying strap. In the old days, the baby would be wrapped and then secured to the board with three straps that wrapped around the body and board: one across the chest under the arms, one across the hips, and one across the knees. Clean cattail fluff, gathered for just that purpose, was used as a "disposal diaper" inside the blankets; a soft leaf was folded into the fluff in such a way that wetness drained away from the baby and to the outside, keeping the baby comfortable while preventing sogginess and diaper rash.

The cradleboard kept the baby secure, safe, and close

to its mother. And also portable. It could be carried, or propped against a tree or rock, or hung from a tree. Small toys or pretties (the great-grandmas of today's mobiles) could be hung from the roll bar. This was the origin of the dreamcatcher, the small spiderweb woven inside a willow hoop, made to capture sweet dreams and keep bad dreams away.

More recent Ojibwe cradleboards have a laced bag secured right to the backboard, which makes it much easier, and faster, to get the baby in and out. Often, the baby and wrappings are covered by a velvet blanket, beaded with Ojibwe-style leaves, vines, and flowers. An Elder lady once told me that the yoke piece of her son's traditional dance outfit had originally been his cradle-board cover, and that when she brought his cradleboard to show to children in an elementary school classroom, she used the yoke again as the cradleboard cover.

Some young Ojibwe mothers still use cradleboards; I have seen them at powwows, at social events, and at the reservation clinic. Every time, the sight catches people's attention. With Ojibwe courtesy, we look gently (and, of course, never stare), smile and nod, and perhaps make some polite conversation with the young mother.

At an Indian education conference a few years ago I met a baby boy who was snug in a cradleboard, propped up in a chair. He was at the conference with his mother and his grandma, whom I have known since our own young mother days. The daughter had made most of the cradleboard herself, with help from her dad; she and her mother had beaded the cover. The largest flowers were edged with orange beads, the leaves with shades of green.

We hadn't seen each other in awhile and had some catching up to do. The baby slept through most of the conversation, in the cradleboard that his grandma had moved from the chair and propped against his mother's knees. His round cheeks pushed his mouth to the shape of a wild rose; the little tuft of hair on the top of his head moved ever so slightly with the rhythm of his light snore. He looked comfortable and secure. And portable.

Memory, Creative Living, and Fun Crocheting from Rags

*a*s I stacked the folded scraps of cotton print leftovers from the last apron I made onto the pile of remnants growing on the shelf in my fabric stash, I was visited by a memory from another time and place not so long ago or very far away.

Our Italian great-grandmother (although we Le-Garde kids were not Italian, it was our good luck to have an Italian great-grandmother-by-marriage), who immigrated to Duluth when she was a teenager, was a woman of an era and culture that took pride and satisfaction in combining the virtue and necessity of thriftiness with creativity and enjoyment. She gardened, kept chickens and pigs, and never wasted anything.

Not even very worn-out and ragged clothing. She mended and patched, reused buttons (which she kept in a jar), and when the clothing was no longer of use turned it into scrub rags, dusting cloths . . . and crocheted rugs.

A childhood memory I love to revisit is sitting next to her watching her tear her husband's and sons' old shirts into long strips that she knotted together and wound into a ball that grew larger and larger. She then began to crochet with an oversized crochet hook, and the ball of rag strips gradually (magically, it seemed to me) changed into a rug shaped in a circle or oval. These she usually gave away to her friends and family.

When I was a little girl we had several of her rugs around the house. The rugs were pretty, absorbent, washable, and held the spirit of women we knew going about their days' work in patterned housedresses, of men in chambray or striped shirts at their labors on work crews and the shoe repair shop. Our mother loved the rugs as she loved the people who had worn the shirts and dresses, and especially the Italian grandmother-by-marriage, who had made them and gifted them to her. When she washed the rugs, she dried them on a clothesline and, when they were nearly dry, set them on the kitchen floor, where she stood, walked, and sometimes stomped and danced them back into their perfect circles or ovals.

Looking at the stack of fabric leftovers and thinking of my mother and our Italian great-grandmother, I thought I would try crocheting rags, but because I didn't feel quite ready to try an entire rug decided on a square hot mat (trivet) for the kitchen table. This is how I, a grandmother in the twenty-first century, went about the task:

I cut fabric scraps into strips approximately three to four inches wide and machine-stitched the strips together, end to end. Tucking in the edges I wound this into a ball that grew larger and larger; later that afternoon my granddaughter Natalie stopped by to visit. When she saw the ball of scraps, she picked it up and held it in her arms. "This is pretty; what is it?" she asked, which again brought lovely memories to my mind. I could see that she thought the ball was a work of art in itself, the way I had thought when I was a little girl. When I answered that I was going to crochet it into a rug or a hot mat, Natalie, who if she were a flower would be a daffodil, looked quite impressed!

It took me only about an hour to make a large hot mat. With my largest crochet hook (the big plastic kind) I began with a chain of twelve stitches, then double-crocheted six rows. When the mat reached about ten by twelve inches, I stopped and single-crocheted around the edges. It is quite thick and should work very well to protect a table from a hot teakettle, saucepan, or hot-dish (casserole dish, for those who aren't originally from here). And in the fabric, knotted from leftover scraps of aprons I have made for women I love, some baby quilts, and cotton sundresses I made for my grown daughters to wear to a wedding a few summers ago, I can see colors and patterns of our history as it continues to unfold.

Migwechiwendam

TO THINK THANKFULLY

Here in Onagamiising, our thoughts turn during the month of November to the beauty of seasonal changes as the Earth prepares to take her winter nap under the lovely white blanket of snow that will soon fall. As we get further into the month we look forward to the Thanksgiving Day holiday and dinner (and children will look forward to the extra excitement of two days off from school!).

Thanksgiving Day is about my favorite day of the year. Onishishin; I think it is wonderful to have an entire national holiday set aside for the purpose of acknowledging blessings and expressing appreciation. I love turkey, stuffing, and wild rice, and love eating it with my family. In recent years my daughters have taken over the preparation of much of the feast, and I have become the Grandma whose family makes sure she has a comfortable chair and doesn't have to do too much work!

As a national holiday, Thanksgiving Day is a com-
memoration of what in school we used to call "The First
Thanksgiving." Of course, that was not the first thanksgiving feast at all. Celebrating the end of the harvest
season and giving thanks to the Creator for the blessings of food, and the beauty of the world, and life, and
each other, have been part of people's lives all over the
world for more centuries than any of us can say. Certainly it was a tradition in the lives of the Native people
whose kind-heartedness saved the lives of the Pilgrims.

In my view the four basic Ojibwe values are gratitude, modesty, generosity, and respect. We understand
that everything in our lives has been provided by the
Creator, that these blessings have made us rich, and that
of course the Creator wants us in turn to be generous
with each other. A good Ojibwe is thankful and endeavors to develop a generous spirit.

When I was a little girl in school we learned about
Squanto the Friendly Indian, who was invited to the
Pilgrims' thanksgiving feast. I recall a picture book that
illustrated the story; inside, Squanto arrived at the feast
carrying a platter of food. Behind him were a couple of
his friends, one carrying a deer over his shoulders and
the other a turkey by its feet. Dressed in loincloths, they
appeared a little thin and chilly in comparison with the
Pilgrims. Because these men looked nothing like any
Indians I had ever seen, I thought the story must have
been fictional.

Many years later I learned the real story.

Tisquantum (whom history has nicknamed Squanto)
was a Patuxet Indian, who as a teenager was kidnapped

by British merchants and brought to England, where his knowledge of his homeland was used for planning other merchant expeditions. An indentured servant, he remained in England for years, working and saving to buy a passage home.

When he arrived home he found that his entire tribe had died, probably of a measles epidemic that started from travelers on a British ship. He found that a number of immigrants who had settled in and near the Patuxet village were experiencing great difficulties, including malnutrition and near-starvation.

In the midst of his own devastation Tisquantum made the choice to help. Other Native people in the area, themselves also remnants of decimated tribes, did the same. Within a year or two the Pilgrims' lives improved dramatically, and a feast was held to celebrate and give thanks. I see brotherhood in the story of the shared feast of thanksgiving; I see extraordinary humanity in the story of the Native people who compassionately shared their knowledge and food with the hopeful immigrants who arrived on this continent so ill-prepared for the climate and terrain.

On Thanksgiving Day, a national holiday and about my favorite day of the year, I will think thankfully of all my blessings and wish good things for my family and yours. I will remember Tisquantum and the Anishinaabeg of all tribes who have responded to life's difficulties with grace and decency, and will try to be like them, of good and generous spirit.

I wish everyone a delicious dinner and a Happy Thanksgiving.

Biboon
Winter

Nanaboozhoo and Nokomis

*d*uring the winter season the Earth sleeps and rests under a soft white blanket of snow. Biboon is a time of reflection, replenishment, and quiet; as our lives move into the wintertime, days grow shorter and nights longer. It grows cold outside; we spend more time indoors, physically closer to one another on dark winter evenings. Biboon is a time to appreciate the closeness of home.

In the old days, during winter evenings at home, Ojibwe families spent more time indoors gathered more closely together in wintertime, too. Physically closer for warmth and company they talked and visited, listened to stories, and worked on what they could indoors: they made and repaired snowshoes, traps, household goods, clothing, and moccasins. Children learned how to do those tasks by watching their elders and paying attention. When it appeared to someone older and wiser

147

that they might have observed and had the maturity and skills to handle the task, they were given the opportunity to try; with practice they became competent and skilled. This was how elders educated and prepared children for when they would become adults, and then elders, themselves; it is how the values and knowledge of the Ojibwe have continued, and why we have them today.

For many generations, winter has been the season for traditional Ojibwe storytelling. The Ojibwe have always been great storytellers who keep and care for stories, telling and passing them down when the time is determined by the storyteller/keeper as appropriate. There are many kinds of stories: romance, adventure, the recounting of history, ghost stories, and the sacred stories, those about creation and how the world came to be the way it is. We wait with patience all year for the return of those sacred stories, told only during the winter, when there is snow on the ground and the small animals are sleeping. Many of these stories involve the spirit hero Nanaboozhoo, who long ago had many adventures as he walked the Earth.

Nanaboozhoo's mother was the granddaughter of the Moon; his father was the North Wind. He is a powerful being who, because he is half-spirit and half-human, has the qualities of both: strengths and weaknesses, wisdom and foolishness. At birth Nanaboozhoo was a small white rabbit who with his tiny twin brother Maingen was orphaned shortly after Maingen's birth, a tragedy that deeply affected them and Nokomis, their grand-

mother. Maingen lived away from their home, and
Nanaboozhoo was raised by Nokomis. One of Nanaboozhoo's superhuman skills is that he has the ability to
change shapes and appearances. He has, at various times
and in various situations, taken the shape of a frog, a
tree trunk, a stone, a duck. In our minds we often picture him as a young man, but that is likely because of
our limitations as human beings.

Nokomis taught Nanaboozhoo everything she knew
about the world and how to live by telling him stories,
letting him watch how things are done, and when the
time was right, letting him try for himself. Of course, in
order for her grandson to truly learn, she had to allow
him space and opportunity to experience life, and to
make his own mistakes. At the same time, she advised
her grandson, watched out for him, and gave him as-
sistance when he needed it. Nokomis is an example and
model for us all as we teach our younger generations.

Guided by the knowledge and example of Nokomis,
as Nanaboozhoo walked the Earth he grew in wisdom.
Today, as our ancestors did, we learn about the world,
and the good ways to be, by hearing the stories about
his life and adventures. The Nanaboozhoo stories are
among the sacred stories told in winter, which is our
season of listening especially carefully. We can relate to
his human qualities, including his wit and his irresistible
joking, his mistakes, and his playing of tricks. Nanaboozhoo stories are awe-inspiring, sad, funny, romantic,
inspirational, spooky, and heartwarming (sometimes all
at once). It is a privilege to hear them, a gift from the

storyteller. If you should have the chance to be at such an occasion, listen quietly, attentively, and with your heart as well as your ears. That is the Ojibwe way.

The darkness and cold of Biboon are designed and planned by the Creator; they have purpose and beauty. I think that in the old days the people began to wonder, when the dark part of the day was so much longer than the hours of light and their children and elders shivered and held one another tightly in body and spirit, how long the food supplies would hold out, and if the family would survive. And then what happened next was just what happens today: in midseason the daylight hours begin to lengthen in preparation, and we can smell a change coming in the cold winter air that is the coming of spring.

Coal, Clinkers, and Staying Warm

*t*he season of Biboon brings quite a lot of snow and cold weather to Onigamiising, and although "up north" is a beautiful place during the winter, we do need to keep an eye on the thermostat and on our heating costs.

We "dial down," put on a sweater, boil water for tea, make a hotdish. (Here's an easy classic: egg noodles cooked al dente; a can of tuna, drained; a can of niblet corn, drained; a can of cream of mushroom soup; a little water. Mix together, place in a greased ovenproof dish, bake at 350 degrees for forty minutes. If you are feeling a little fancy, crumble some potato chips or crackers on top before you put it in the oven. Don't let it dry out; cover it if, like me, you worry about this.)

As the kitchen warms up we listen, often unconsciously, for any irregularities in the smooth running of the heating system.

My brother Jerry called me the other day to chat

about The Furnace. He was referring to the large, round, octopus-armed coal furnace that took up the middle of the basement when we were kids. For my brother, his responsibilities with The Furnace and keeping the house warm were a big part of wintertime (that, and his paper route).

Our dad got things ready in the morning, with coal in the stoker that would last the day, but after school it was Jerry's job to clean out the cinder and clinker pan. And to shovel some coal into the stoker, if it looked to be running out.

I reminded Jerry that our mom and dad were pretty happy to see that the house they'd bought had an electric stoker that fed coal into the furnace throughout the day ("a worm feeder," Jerry affirmed); this was a great convenience. Before that, the furnace had to be banked twice a day, early in the morning and right before bedtime.

Jerry turned the subject back to clinkers, and the disposing of clinkers into the yard, and then the picking of clinkers out of the yard in the spring and summer.

"What is a clinker, anyway?" I asked.

He told me that the coal we burned, from Montana, had a high metal content, and that intense heat fused some small parts of it into metal lumps. "I always thought they looked so pretty and shiny when you put them in the snow," I said, "like melted silver." A polite silence on his end, from the boy who had spent his preteen and adolescent years on clinker duty.

"Do you remember when they delivered coal and poured it down a chute into the coal bin?" he asked.

"And do you remember when people didn't have enough money for that, they could buy a two-by-four-foot bag of coal?"

I did.

And we remembered, too, the warmth of our house on winter mornings: our mother cooking oatmeal; we girls ironing our dad's workshirts and our dresses, skirts, and blouses; and the little kids wrapped cozily in blankets and watching *Captain Kangaroo* on TV while the rest of us got ready for school. I suppose the house must have been chilly at times, but we didn't remember feeling really cold.

When I told my husband that Jerry and I had been talking about The Furnace, and about clinkers, he was reminded of a job he'd had when he was a kid, in Aitkin: cleaning clinkers every Saturday afternoon from the furnace in the basement of a downtown store, and then using them to fill potholes in the alley. I guess there must be a lot of guys of that age with clinker stories.

It's funny how the mention of a small piece of melted and fused metal brings it all back, just like that.

Trying to Make Lugalette like My Grandmother

i have had enough practice making frybread that it turns out most of the time: the dough puffs are golden, the texture consistent and very slightly sweet from that scant teaspoonful of sugar that I add to the flour. I don't make it as often as I used to, but I remember that whenever I did my dad always made a point of telling me that it was good. It must have reminded him of something else his mother, my grandmother Vicky, used to make: lugalette.

"We always thought that the word was so funny, LUGGL-ett," he said.

Like frybread, the recipes for and customs of making lugalette have varied from family to family. Some pronounce it "lug-o-lay," and to others it is called "Indian bread" or "lug bread" or just plain "lug." It is not as well known as frybread; it was probably made and eaten more in the old days than today.

Frybread (which we used to cook in lard) is deep-fried in oil or shortening, which adds to the cost. Lugalette is baked in a pan and so uses a very small amount of grease. My dad, who was a child during the Great Depression, has told me that they had it at home every day. I am sure that was so for many people during those difficult times. His memory of this, though, was not that people were so poor that they filled up on lugalette, but that it smelled so good and was so delicious.

In honor of my grandmother, I have tried to re-create her lugalette recipe—with some help from my dad's recollections of watching her cook. Here is what he remembered.

Grandmother Vicky would take enough flour to fill a mixing bowl somewhat less than halfway up. She would mix in some baking powder that she measured into the middle of her hand, and then a little salt and a small handful of sugar. She mixed in some warm water and kept the dough soft. She kneaded it just a little, then put it into a greased pan, and flattened it very gently with the palms of her hands. She baked it and sliced it.

The lugalette my dad remembered was served hot or cold, and usually plain. Sometimes, though, his mother mixed some blueberries or raspberries in before she baked it; sometimes she served it with a little maple syrup poured on top. I think it would be good with a little butter and honey.

The first time I tried to make lugalette it was not good at all. I have experimented and learned to keep a tender hand with the dough. I don't believe they make a pan the size that my grandmother used; my dad remembered the pan as rectangular, and smaller than an eight-by-eleven-inch cake pan. It was wider than a loaf pan, he said. I have used an eight-by-eight-inch cake pan but think that a narrower one would give a better texture to the center. Loaf pans are just too narrow; I have found that lugalette works out best if the dough is only an inch or so high.

Lugalette does not have the melt-in-your-mouth crust that comes of deep-frying, and in that way it really does differ from frybread. It is from a different era—I suppose it might be frybread's grandmother or auntie. For me, making good lugalette is a challenge, but I'll keep practicing. The texture of dough on my hands makes me think of my grandmother, and of my dad as a boy, eating lugalette that he remembered smelled so good and was so delicious.

Snow Shoveling, Chocolate,
and a Pretty Kitchen

*m*ino giizhigad," I thought one winter morning as I looked out the kitchen window. It looked like it was going to be a good day: outside the sun was shining, chickadees were diving from the garage to the trees and back to the bird feeder, and overnight it had snowed about an inch or two of snow as delicate looking as Chantilly lace over a graying snowbank. Everything looked clean, including the back porch and stairs that needed shoveling.

I don't shovel as much as I used to (one reason is our grandson, who lives with us), but I have always enjoyed clearing up the kind of fresh snow that is so light that it flies like dandelion fluff as I throw it over the bank. That morning I borrowed my husband's lightweight fleece jacket, paired with one of his stocking hats—a good shoveling outfit. When I got outside the lady next door was out shoveling, too. She was wearing her hooded jacket and her pac boots and watching for the mailman. We waved, as we always do.

The two of us, the lady next door and myself, make me think of my Aunt Vicky and her next-door neighbor shoveling on nice winter days, quite a few years ago. I remember them clearing their sidewalks and stairs, and then sweeping their front porches clean. To shovel, Aunt Vicky wore a long coat, mittens, rubber boots with a strip of synthetic fur around the top, and a wool kerchief, with her hair neatly combed into white scallops that framed her forehead. She looked nearly as dressed up shoveling as she did for church, or for a Transit Wednesday shopping trip downtown. For those occasions she and her friends wore nice hats and gloves.

Because my aunt was elderly and lived alone, when there was more than just a little dusting of snow we went to shovel for her. She was always so happy to see us: she thanked us and told my little brothers how strong they were. She would have us in for cocoa, then, to warm up. Her kitchen was so pretty: my dad had painted the walls baby blue and had drawn wavy pink stripes on the ceiling tiles. She served our cocoa in the same nice cups that the grownups used. Every visit looked like a party. We were always treated like company.

Last weekend, on another pretty morning with some overnight snow, our daughter and her husband brought their family over to clear the back porch, stairs, and sidewalk. The older children shoveled; I told them what a big help they were, how strong they were. The youngest wanted to help, too, and because there weren't enough shovels I had her sweep the snow off the back porch as I shook out the mat. First, though, she had to put on her snowpants. She told me she doesn't like their puffiness. I told her about the snowpants I wore when I was a little girl, the big blue wool ones that made me look like a stuffed toy. "When they got wet, Grandma Pat hung them over the heat register," I said. "They smelled like a wet dog!" We laughed and laughed; the snow flew from the porch.

When the grandchildren were finished helping, they came inside for cocoa and toast. Their cheeks were healthily pink, their eyes bright and shiny, their noses a little drippy. And their snowpants and jackets wet; we hung them on chairbacks over the heat registers to dry.

As they sat at the kitchen table stirring marshmallows around in their cocoa and dunking their toast, Lindsay, the middle child who if she were a flower would be a rose, admired the row of little antique dishes that I had hung on the wall. "It sure is pretty in here, Grandma," she said.

A memory was being made, as memories were made when I was a child. Onishishin.

Storytelling Seasons

i n Ojibwe tradition, wintertime is the season for storytelling. Just last week I was thinking about one of my
favorite stories, the one about how Gaagoons, the little
porcupine, scares off some bullies with help from our
spirit hero, Nanaboozhoo. What I especially love about
this story is that Gaagoons maintains his exemplary gentle and kindly ways after he becomes a great warrior.

Ojibwe stories about creation and how the world
came to be are sacred stories and are told only when
there is snow on the ground. This tradition, like the
stories, has been passed from generation to generation
for many years, and we continue to honor it. One reason, I have been told, is that some of the stories involve
animals that are sleeping during the wintertime months
and so they won't hear us talking about them; we are
being considerate of their feelings. In keeping with this
wintertime tradition we also honor the ancestors who

took care to learn the stories and pass them down. We honor spiritual teachings and our own survival as a people. We honor the stories themselves as living entities.

There are many Native tribes, and each has its own spiritual and cultural ways and customs. Even among the Ojibwe there are differences in stories among reservations, bands, communities, clans, and families. An experience I had on a very hot July evening several years ago reminded me of this.

I was visiting in South Carolina and was invited to a powwow and feast at the Catawba reservation. Because those lands had only recently and after a very long struggle been returned to the tribe, the Catawbas were working very hard on connecting their spiritual customs and traditions to their ancestors' homeland. Part of this effort was a tribal building and powwow grounds.

I was invited to a celebration at the tribal building, a remodeled community club they had moved onto reservation land. For the feast they served a traditional quail pie; how fragrant it was, and how tender the crust and meat. This was an old-time dish that some of the elders had re-created from their childhood memories, someone told me; through trial and error, and many taste testings, they thought they had the gravy just right. The elders looked so happy and proud as everyone praised the wonderful quail pie. The ladies who were overseeing the serving. And the men who were carrying the heavy trays made sure that everyone got a piece—everyone was very polite about not taking more than their share; just the same, there were no leftovers!

After we ate, younger people cleared the dishes as we

went outside to wait for one of the Catawba elders who wished to share a story with us. This was quite a new experience for me, sitting under the very hot summer sun to hear a native sacred story. At first, it felt strange. A young woman brought me a glass of water and asked how I was holding up in the heat. If I got too warm it would be okay to go inside the tribal building, she told me. Everyone would understand and nobody would be offended.

The storyteller, a Catawba elder who had been pre-paring in the woods for this special occasion—he had been saying prayers and offering tobacco—emerged from a stand of trees and began to talk. Aware of the tremendous work it had taken to maintain Catawba tra-dition and to restore Catawba land, everyone listened very closely, even the smallest children, who sat in their parents' laps. As I listened I also watched the storyteller and the appreciative faces of the listeners, which re-minded me of what a beautiful and diverse world this is.

After the storytelling, the Catawba people and we their guests danced with joy and thanks at the pow-wow. We had such a good time that I forgot about the heat as I danced with a line of traditional Catawba women, matching my steps to theirs.

I think about the Catawba people often and how, like the Ojibwe, they honor and appreciate their tradi-tions, land, and elders, sharing the best of everything they have with their guests. Perhaps one day I will be able to visit there again and hear another story. In the meantime . . .

Here in Onigamiising, when there is snow on the ground, it will be the season of Biboon, wintertime, and we will be in storytelling season. Every year I wait for the opportunity to tell my favorite story, the one about Gaagoons. And maybe one or two more. Before the snow melts away.

A Soldier on Leave

*W*e watched the children at our house while the sergeant's wife, our daughter, drove to the airport to
meet her husband's plane. For what must have seemed
a very, very long hour, the three stayed close to the
front room window, keeping the street and driveway
in sight.

"What are they doing right now?" the first grader
asked every seven minutes or so.

I answered each time with something new. He was
in the plane getting closer to Duluth. He was, perhaps,
right over Cloquet, over Lake Superior, over the Aerial
Bridge. Right now the plane was probably landing.
Their mother was waiting for the passengers to come
through the door. They might be getting in the car
right now; they might be on their way to our house
from the airport.

The third grader thought he would be surprised to

see all the snow. Yes, my husband answered; remember how the day he left for Afghanistan was sunny and warm?

The sixth grader waited in the recliner next to the window and was the first to spot the van. We watched him let his little sisters run outside to the driveway (the first grader without her shoes) ahead of him.

Once inside the back door, the sergeant looked around (while his wife held his arm). "It seems so strange to be in a house," he commented, having spent six months in a tent. We asked if we could take them out to eat, and where they'd like to go. The sergeant chose the Ground Round, where he savored each and every bite of his burger and fries, and every word of conversation.

When I was a child, two weeks was the length of Christmas vacation. It was one-sixth of summer vacation. On a day when I was nearly eight, my mother showed me that my birthday was exactly two weeks away. Two weeks was a very long time, indeed.

I am sure that to my grandchildren, the two-week leave that came just over halfway through their dad's lengthy deployment seemed on that first day quite a lengthy stretch. I hope that it seemed as long to them as Christmas vacation did to me when I was their age.

Here is some of what filled our soldier's two-week leave. Visiting relatives: Grandma, Dad, in-laws, brothers, nieces and nephews, cousins.

Petting the dog (who thinks the sergeant is his dad). Walking the dog, feeding the dog, playing with the dog, sitting by the dog, allowing the dog to show his devotion by lying on the sergeant's feet while he watched TV.

Remembering how to drive over ice and snow.

Driving the kids to school and picking them up. Visiting and speaking to a sixth-grade social studies classroom.

Going to church.

Having a steak dinner date with his wife. Enjoying a night on the town with friends and relatives, some visiting from Warroad.

Catching up on sleep. Catching up on chores around the house. Cooking, doing laundry.

Checking out the van to make sure everything was in good running shape for the second half of his deployment.

Enjoying every single minute, even, as he mentioned on Facebook, listening to his kids argue.

At the end of the two weeks our daughter drove him by herself to the airport. She and the kids, and the dog, too, were very quiet for the next week as they got back into their pre-leave routine of life. They went about the business of everyday life: going to school, to work, to the library, to church. They went to the mall for new shoes, to a friend's house to play. And they waited.

They missed him; we all did. We are just one of many families who have had someone serving our country. We are proud of what they do for us, and thankful. As a man I work with said about his son who deployed, "He does his job so that I can do mine."

"Just think, when your dad comes back it will be warm summer weather," I said to the little girls during the long second half of his absence. "Won't he be surprised to see that the snow is all gone?" Their faces perked up, as they always did when someone mentioned their dad, during what must have seemed an unimaginably long time. Just as we did during the hour's wait while our daughter went to the airport to pick him up for his leave, we segmented time, marked it by event and season. Every day, we said every day, is one day closer to when he comes home.

The dog waited, too. He had no idea how long it was going to be but knew that his job was to take good care of the sergeant's family and keep them company.

Cold Feet and New Beginnings

*M*any of us begin the month of January by celebrating the start of a New Year. We visit with friends and family, enjoy a nice meal, and make resolutions to change our lifestyles for the better (well, as I said, "many"—I will admit that I haven't ever made a New Year's resolution, but that doesn't mean I won't someday).

We think of January as a month of new beginnings, of fresh chances and starts. The Earth herself must feel this, too: on January 1, New Year's Day, we are ten days past the longest night of the year. Every day there are more hours of sunlight, and by the end of January we can really see and feel this.

When I am out in January weather I appreciate my boots: although they are old enough to be in the second or third grade, they are in pretty good shape, with solid treads, and they keep my feet warm almost all the time.

When it gets to be twenty-five below zero and my feet feel cold, I still feel lucky to have them, and as so often happens, a story comes to mind; distracted then, I forget about the cold.

The story: it was during the cold January not long after I turned eighteen that I walked the cold, icy sidewalks of downtown Duluth looking for a job. I had recently left school at UMD after an unsuccessful (that is a euphemism for mostly failed) quarter of college, my left boot had sprung a leak, and my spirit was as dampened and cold as my feet. I had filled out many job applications, but I think that the sad, discouraged expression on my face, my fingers that reddened and became clumsy as they thawed, and my bitten-down nails gave a less-than-confident and competent impression.

As the sky darkened I made one last stop at the storefront personnel office of Northwestern Bell, on Fourth Avenue West. The woman behind the desk didn't seem to notice that I was shivering, that my nose was red, and my cold fingers stiff as I held the pencil to fill out the application and the aptitude test. "This looks good," she said, briefly eyeballing the test. "We'll call you if we would like you to come in for an interview. We're hiring." The bedraggled wings of my spirit lifted ever so tentatively.

I rode the bus home with a neighbor lady, who asked me how college was going. I had to tell her. She said, so sympathetically, "O-hhh, so here you were downtown all day looking for work, with a cold foot." We half-laughed. "You'll find a nice job," she said.

Miraculously, it seemed, she was right. Northwest-

ern Bell called me for an interview, and in that January
of new beginnings I was hired for my first real job, a toll
(long distance) operator. As Operator 36 I learned how
to set up calls on the cord board, connecting mothers
to their sons on army bases, elderly shut-ins to the Busy
Bee Market for grocery orders, shore calls to Great
Lakes ships, frightened people with emergencies to
the police and fire departments (this was before 911). I
learned to work in very close physical proximity to the
operators on either side of me, to cooperatively criss-
cross our cords over each other's work, to trade shifts
and days off, to get to the switchboard five minutes
early in consideration for the operator I would replace.
I learned to take pride in my work, and I developed a
work ethic (at times reluctantly, but I learned) as well as
a respect for the honor of all work and workers.

When I was hired at Bell in January 1969, the super-
visor told me that I was learning a skill that would serve
me well, that I would be able to find a job all the rest
of my life. Ten years after that fresh start and second
chance, changing technologies closed switchboards and
operators were no longer needed. Yet I found that what
I learned about work at Bell did indeed serve me well
in all the diverse jobs I have had since then. I am still
Operator 36.

A Rabbit Skin Baby Blanket

*t*he word for waboos in English is "rabbit."

Waboos appears regularly in the Ojibwe stories that teach us about how the world came to be the way it is today. He was there when Nanaboozhoo, who had begun life as a tiny white rabbit, brought fire to the Ojibwe; he managed to keep from laughing as Nanaboozhoo through some foolish decisions learned not to be selfish with food; he watched his little son learn, painfully, not to brag but to be modest, helpful to others, and brave. Countless generations of Ojibwe children have learned by listening to their elders tell and retell the stories that their own elders told to them when they were children themselves. Waboos is part of the Ojibwe oral tradition that guides us in the direction of Mino-bimaadiziwin, the living of a good life.

Waboos has also provided physical gifts of food and warmth to Ojibwe people. This is part of his destiny and one of the reasons he was created. In our prayers before we eat rabbit meat we thank the Creator and also the spirit of Waboos, acknowledging that a life has been given up for our existence. This prayer of thanks continues as we respectfully try to not waste anything but make the best use of the rest of the rabbit, including his lovely soft fur.

As a young mother I worked for the Indian Education program in Hibbing, Minnesota, up north on the Iron Range; there I learned many things. The program and the superintendent of schools were advised by what was informally called the Parent Committee, a grass-roots group that met once a month. Some of us brought our children to meetings; at one of these a grandmother was admiring my baby daughter, Abby, and the lacy acrylic shawl I had draped across her infant carrier. The open work white yarn reminded her a little of those rabbit skin baby blankets that the old-time Ojibwe used to make, she said. Had I ever seen one?

I had not. How were they made? I asked. And she became animated as she described the making of the blanket.

"I don't think it's that hard to do. You'd have to get together about forty rabbit skins, but look—you've already got three." This was true; we used them like doilies, on a table that displayed some birchbark baskets. "It goes like this . . ."

As she spoke she motioned with her hands to show how she remembered an older lady, perhaps her own grandmother, weave a rabbit skin baby blanket. I could almost picture the makings of the blanket in her lap.

Today I recall four things about that afternoon: my brown-eyed baby with a complexion like a peach; the lacy white baby shawl (a gift from one of my relatives); the happy, crow's feet–framed eyes of the grandmother who passed on to me a memory from her girlhood; and (perhaps not as clearly) the instructions for making an old-time Ojibwe rabbit skin blanket. Here they are:

You will need forty to fifty air-tanned rabbit skins (white or very light colors work well for a baby blanket). Starting from the outside edge, cut each skin into inch-wide strips going round and round in a spiral until you get to the center. This will give you a strip that is probably five feet or more in length. As you cut in the spiral direction, each strip will curl and give, creating a furry surface all around the strip. Begin your blanket by laying out the first strip as long as you would want the blanket to be wide, then go back over that strip in another spiral, like a candy cane, that leaves a series of little scallops. At the end of the row, go back again by weaving the strip in a little loop through each scallop. Do this row by row until the blanket is the length you want. When you reach the end, you can do a single crochet along all four sides to give it a little more defined shape.

Now, here is some important information about the adding on of each strip. You only need to add one strip at a time (otherwise your work will become cumbersome and difficult to handle). One way to do this is to cut a tiny hole at the end of each strip. Before you start with the first strip, string the end of it through its own hole, which will then make a loop. When you are ready to add a strip, you will string and secure it through the loop at the end of the string before it; each will have its own loop. This sounds complicated, but it does create a neat blanket. Another option would be to hand-sew each new strip onto the previous one. Again, not all at once.

I never did make a rabbit skin blanket, but years later in Canada I saw one made by an Ojibwe woman who had learned the art. She let me look closely at the weave, the edging, and the looped-together strips of fur. The blanket, of Nanaboozhoo-white rabbit fur, was as soft and lightweight as the one that the grandmother had described to me that afternoon when Abby was a baby.

"It's beautiful," I said. "I sure admire you for learning to do this."

Her reply was appropriately Ojibwe-like, modest, and proud. "Migwech; it took some patience but it turned out better than I thought."

Perhaps the baby who received that soft, lacey-looking white rabbit skin blanket had brown eyes and a complexion like a peach.

The Gift and Privilege
of Parenting

*I*t came up in the middle of a conversation about our cars' block heaters, her daughter's English class, and a fundraiser event at school. With some concern in her voice, one of my daughters mentioned to me that she is "still learning" how to parent her two children, who are in their teens. She seemed to be wondering if she should have it all figured out by now. Her soft voice and questioning spirit touched my heart; I hope that my reply, brief as it was, supported and strengthened the wonderful job she is doing raising those girls.

I, too, am still learning how to parent, and as my three grown daughters journey through their lives as mothers, I watch them experience some things that are familiar to me (like reminding the abinoojiiyag to look both ways before crossing the street, and planning for jackets that will fit for two winters and stay in good shape to pass to another child) and some that are not (like overseeing their use of the Internet).

Parenting, and grandparenting also, isn't always easy, but it is always a gift. It is joy and pleasure as well as a challenge and hard work to have young spirits in our lives, and a privilege that I believe Native people very consciously and deliberately don't take for granted. My grandmother, and her grandmother too, both experienced the loss of very young children to the federal Indian boarding school system. That absence continued through the time those children finished or left school.

The Indian boarding school era officially lasted from 1879 to 1934; however, some boarding schools existed in America since before 1600, and the dismantling of the system, which began under the Indian Reorganization Act of 1934, took decades to more or less complete. Boarding schools, and the policies that supported them, caused tremendous damage to American Indian families as well as disruption in the passing of traditions, knowledge, and spiritual beliefs and practices from generation to generation.

So many effects of the historical trauma, which is also called by a more fitting name, intergenerational trauma, caused by the Indian boarding school experience are still with us today; however, I believe that such upheaval and loss led our tenacious ancestors to pass on to us a profound appreciation for children and for our extended families. From time to time as I pass family stories along to my young relatives I mention some of our grandparents' (and my parents' and my own) experiences at school. Sometimes these stories have simple and happy endings; more often they are complicated and filled with the untidiness of life here on Mother Earth; all are connected to the lives of other extended family members and friends.

And all have a common, unspoken thread running throughout: the survival of a people and the continuity of our collective story and knowledge through the oral tradition. Children are the gift that makes this possible: our task is to care for them and treasure them in preparation for the day they will become the tellers of the story to new generations.

Parenting isn't easy, but when it gets to be hard, I hope that young parents will take heart in remembering that the legacy of their ancestors, the boarding school children, surely includes a force of spirit and intergenerational love, and that they will feel strengthened.

I didn't say all of this to my daughter; I believe that she already knows much more than she realizes. My reply was that she does a good job, she is a great mother with great kids, and that we are all figuring out things as we go along. It is important for her to hear this and important for her to experience things for herself in her own life journey. For the rest of the answer, she will continue to learn and to teach, as she starts her cold car in the morning to go to work ("So, do I need to get a new block heater, do you think?"); as she reads her daughter's English assignments; as she gives her time and talent to the school fundraiser.

Parenting isn't easy, but she knows our history and doesn't take the gift for granted. Cared for and treasured, her girls are being prepared for their part in the continuation of our survival and story. Gaye onishishin.

A Cousin Gets in Touch
with a Cousin

*a*t our house the Internet arrived sometime during the mid-1990s, and it was quite a wonder. I can remember getting on the World Wide Web to access information for a paper I was writing for a class. How amazing it was to do homework research while sitting at home drinking cocoa! I called my dad, who enjoyed marveling at new inventions and ways of doing things, to share the experience. What would they think of next?—Two-way wrist radios? A space coupe? we joked—remembering the technological gadgets in the Dick Tracy cartoon strip.

Now, of course, even small children use the Internet with ease, but I still marvel over the ways in which technologies can bring so much of the world to the screen in front of us. I usually think of this as a massive amount of ever-expanding information that seems to distance us from each other the more we learn; how-

ever, once in awhile the Internet has made possible a
return to something much closer to home: the reveal-
ing of connections between relatives who over the years
and through family historical experiences and events
have lost touch.

Last fall I opened my e-mail to a question from
a woman who lives out of state, a long ways from
Onigamiising. She had read my books, she said; she
wondered about my maiden name, LeGarde, and did
a little more Internet research. It looked as though our
families might have intersected a few generations ago.
Could we be related?

We are, and we are cousins. Outside of Indian Country the term *removed* is used to note and identify specific
degrees of cousinhood, but the way this works among
Ojibwe is that we are, simply, cousins. We are of course
very interested in the complexities of who is related to
whom, and how: this ongoing discussion takes place
at every powwow, ceremony, and social gathering.
We address blood relatives of our peer generations,
and sometimes beloved people who aren't technically
blood related, as *cousin*. It is a term of recognition and
acknowledgment that is also a term of endearment.

People lose touch with families and family members
through diverse circumstances, and as we see in televi-
sion advertisements for genealogical resources, people
find and rediscover relatives every day. For American
Indian people there are particular historical factors that
have complicated the search for one's relatives. One of
these is the Indian boarding school system, which is the
one that separated my cousin's family and mine long

ago and now, decades later, reconnects us within the circle of cousins.

The boarding school system, designed to obliterate Native language, religious beliefs, and way of life, did quite a destructive job on many families. Indian boarding school was the point at which the link that held her family and mine together became stressed beyond its ability to hold, and broke. We are thankful for those who didn't break and carried and cared for much (but not all) of that tribal knowledge; we mourn and honor the memories of those who didn't make it.

And we wonder, too, about the effects of historical trauma that are now recognized as intergenerational trauma, and how we might ever come to terms with it.

My oshkii-cousin touched on some of these things in our brief exchange of e-mails. She hopes that she might learn more, and that in doing so she might gain some understanding. I feel the same way. This would not have happened if the Internet, in its never-ending crisscrossing of information, had not interwoven the searching and wondering of two boarding school descendants, lost and now newly found cousins.

She plans to travel up this way; I really hope that we can meet and spend time together. There is a great deal that we will of course never know and will always wonder about, all our lives, yet I know that our bond of history and blood strengthens us. We are Anishinaabeikwewag, after all, descendants of people whose lives, difficult though they were in so many ways, were also beautiful and graced and blessed the Earth.

Henry Meets Santa Claus

*b*iboon Bimaadizimin, the AICHO (American Indian Community Housing Organization) holiday season craft show and bazaar, is always a fun gathering as well as a great opportunity to support local artists and crafters, try delicious foods, and socialize with friends and neighbors. It is held in Trepanier Hall, on Second Street. Trepanier adjoins the AICHO apartments/services building, which is the old YWCA building.

For the past few years I have set up shop at Biboon Bimaadizimin, usually with at least one of my daughters. At our table we sell aprons, books, handmade knitted doll hats, stuffed toys, and, one year, a stack of my grandson's wrestling magazines (the wrestling magazines went really fast). We sold some things, bought Christmas presents, visited, and ate frybread with blueberry sauce (I suppose we smiled at our customers with blue teeth for the rest of the day).

Among the visitors at Biboon Bimaadizimin, small children especially seem to appreciate the holiday crafts and decorations that so many of the vendors displayed. One little boy pointed out a Christmas tree decorated with handcrafted ornaments to his toddler-age sister, and then a crocheted Santa Claus decoration. I heard him say "Santa" several times, speaking with the happiness of knowing a wonderful and certain truth. And I thought of another little boy, this one now an adult, at a Christmas party that the UMD Anishinaabe Club students hosted for children some years ago.

The little guy, Henry, came along with his mother and his uncle, who was going to put on a Santa Claus costume and give out gifts that the students had bought for the children. Henry was quite pleased to be made such a fuss over by the college girls who brought him Christmas cookies and sat with him on the couch (he didn't seem to notice at all that his uncle was no longer present), and he really got into the music as the students swung into "Santa Claus Is Coming to Town." While the children weren't watching, two of us went to escort the good man from the Indian Studies office next door. Hoisting his black plastic sack, he looked as excited as a kid.

"Wait, wait a second!" Another student, who had left the room a few minutes earlier, was hurrying down the hall to catch up to Santa. "We're short a present! Here, this one is for Henry!" The students, who were on a tight budget, had carefully counted the number of children who came through the door; Henry was the last child in, and the smallest. From a UMD bookstore bag she pulled a teddy bear with a message board on its stomach and a marker attached by a ribbon. "The bookstore was just closing, and we're out of wrapping paper." She wrote "HENRY" on the bear's stomach and put it back in the UMD bag, which she put at the top of Santa's sack.

Santa Claus sat in the chair of honor, next to a bowl of candy canes. The students, children, and parents looked expectant, especially Henry, whose mother held him in her lap (perhaps ready to distract him in case there wasn't a gift for an unexpected guest). Santa ho-ho-hoed and opened his sack, lifting out the UMD bag. "The first one's for . . ." (he looked into the bag and then held it out) ". . . Henry!"

Henry climbed down from his mother's lap and walked to the front of the room to get his gift, smiling hugely when he recognized his name, written by the great man himself (that beaming Santa with the twinkling brown eyes, unrecognized by Henry) right on the bear's stomach! There hadn't been any doubt in his mind; of course Santa would bring him a gift.

At Biiboon Bimaadizimin, the "good life in winter" seasonal arts and crafts event, we gather, *giinawind,* old families and new ones, too, Anishinaabeg and our honored guests. Among us will be small children whose belief in Santa will add a sparkle to the day, and to our hearts. We will shop, visit, eat, perhaps buy a crocheted and magical Santa Claus ornament, knowing that all of it, every bit, is part of Onigamiising bimaadiziwin, the living of a good life here in the place of the small portage.

Toot-Cair

*t*o the people of my father's generation, New Year's Day was a day of celebration, one of the most anticipated days of the year. I don't know when this was integrated into Ojibwe tradition, but elders talk from time to time about the fun they used to have. On this day of new beginnings we still think back on the old days and anticipate the new. Some of us will make New Year's resolutions. This might be the year that we reflect on those core Ojibwe values of respect, modesty, generosity, and gratitude, and how we will try to live Mino-bimaadiziwin, the good life, every day. For the Ojibwe of my father's generation, New Year's Day was an occasion to visit relatives, a house-to-house intergenerational celebration of saying "Boozhoo!" shaking hands and kissing cheeks. In the midst of a season when obtaining enough food and heat were often difficult, the people put their cares aside for the day of celebration.

My husband's French Canadian family observed a long-standing custom of their people on New Year's Day by feasting on a special good-luck dish made from a recipe handed down from family to family. One year I decided to try combining the Ojibwe custom of house-to-house visiting with that French Canadian custom of beginning the year with that special meat pie dinner. I made meat pies in honor of Tim and of those New Year's Days not so long ago, when we sat at his family's table and started the year off right with this good-luck meal.

My father-in-law called this pie "toot-cair," and my mother-in-law learned how to make it from her mother-in-law, Artense DuCharme. My mother-in-law followed the DuCharme recipe: her toot-cair was a double crust (made with lard, so that it was very tender) filled with fried ground pork, mashed potato, onion, and spices. It had a crumbly texture and tasted ever so slightly and tantalizingly of nutmeg.

The DuCharme dynasty descendants have enjoyed their New Year's Day toot-cair for many, many decades before they even moved to the Prairie du Chien fur trade town in 1850. The original name for this dish, *tourtiere,* is French; the pronunciation has changed somewhat over the years, in a way similar to how some words in Ojibwe language have modified.

Although changes in our language, as well as in our lives, have not always been our choice, adaptation and sometimes compromise have been a necessity for survival. Sometimes adaptation can even lead to something better. That was my hope for my first try at toot-cair, modified to make it compatible with my cooking abilities.

I used shortening in my pie crust, and instead of fried pork I cooked two roasts, one pork and one beef, which I cut into very small pieces and mixed with potatoes cut very small and boiled to softness. I made four deep-dish pies: two pork-and-potato and two beef-and-potato, with no spices at all, no onion, and put out the salt and pepper shakers in order that people might season their servings to their own tastes.

I thought the pies turned out pretty well: the crusts were tender, not soggy on the bottom at all, and the meat and potatoes held together so that they sliced well. They were more like pasties than toot-cair; however, my husband seemed really touched and pleased that I would do this. Although I noticed that he salted and peppered generously, he considerately did not say that they weren't much like his mother's at all.

Since that first attempt I have talked with a couple of highly experienced cooks, who advised me to either grind the meat or chop it very fine, and to mix the meat with *lumpy* mashed potatoes to give the pies a traditional texture and cohesiveness. An elderly lady seemed to be trying not to laugh as she explained that toot-cair really needs some onion and spices.

My Aunt Peggy mailed me a recipe for Canadian Meat Pie and the words to a little song. This recipe recommends ground game meat, diced potatoes, sage, cinnamon, and cloves. The happy song is from the Pastor of the Times Square Church in New York. He is a former Canadian police officer. The last lines are "Mother has a recipe, Grandma has one too; the only thing that would make it better is sharing a piece with you!"

The next time that I make toot-cair, my daughters and their families will visit, in the Ojibwe custom, while the pies are in the oven. We will wish each other a Happy New Year and start the year with a slice of French Canadian toot-cair. Sometime I might adapt even further and make a pie with venison or rabbit. Now, that would really be an Ojibwe Toot-Cair.

May we all have a Minwendam Anamikoodading, a Happy New Year, every year.

Memories Rose like
Fabric-scented Steam

*a*s an old friend and I walked together at the mall, he mentioned a woman he knows, who told him that when she irons, the scent of hot cloth and steam rising brings her vivid memories of pressing her brother's army uniform before he left home. Further chapters of the story, of what happened next in their young lives, return also; as she irons, she remembers.

"Think of that," he said. "What just that one thing, the smell of ironing, can bring back; so many things, if you think about it." Our conversation turned to that, the smell of ironing and some things that we remembered. And he was right, there are many.

When I was a girl the ironing board was set up at the bottom of the stairs, in the middle of the house. Mornings, we took turns pressing out skirts and dresses, and my dad's paint shirts. My dad was a house painter; every day he wore a clean white dress shirt that was neatly ironed by one of his daughters. These shirts, bought used at the Goodwill or Used-a-Bit, got to be pretty full of paint after a few wearings; we learned that old paint specks could be ironed right over, but larger and fresher smears could melt into the iron. For those we turned the shirt over and used an old dishtowel as a pressing cloth underneath. Cotton shirts stayed crisp longer, I remember, as they hung on the back of the dining room chair; heated, Dacron shirts smelled sweet but then drooped a little limply as they cooled. We liked doing this little task for our dad.

What else does just thinking about that ironing smell bring to mind? Learning to iron by pressing handkerchiefs when I was little, and my mother giving me two nickels for the work (I was proud of the pile of hankies and of earning money, too). My sister draping a miniskirt over the board, measuring for a hem, pinning, pressing before she stitched, the iron sputtering steam. Stubbing my little toe on the ironing board leg as I ran down the stairs, ready for school, making a dramatic fuss, my mother telling me to be more careful. A girlfriend who got up early winter mornings to iron because it felt so good to warm up there in the kitchen with the iron hissing and the coffeepot belching on the stove. Learning to sew with the "press as you go" method, which made for a neater garment and actually saved time and work. The sprinkler bottle, which was a used pop bottle with a nifty little cork/sprinkler. Do you remember "sprinkling" clothes?

Here are a few more ironing board memories. Pressing bright autumn leaves between sheets of waxed paper (use an old dishtowel both above and below, to keep the iron and the ironing board cover clean), then hanging them in the window, where the afternoon sun lit them to a stained-glass effect. The very smoothly ironed dollars tucked in birthday cards from our Grandma Carmie. Lightly, delicately touching up my daughter's wedding veil, just hours before she was a bride. The almost invisible sheen pressed into the BDUs my daughter, the teenaged married lady, ironed for her husband, a young Army National Guard private, to wear standing guard at the Duluth airport in the months after 9/11. I watched footage of him doing this on the news; he looked strong, serious, humbly proud to serve. And very young.

That's all it took, just a small question from an old friend: memories rose like fabric-scented steam from an ironing board. And now I have been blessed with another, this one of walking at the mall with an old friend. As he said, "Just that one thing, the smell of ironing, can bring back so many things, if you think about it."

Cheeseburgers for Breakfast

*L*ike many Duluthians of my generation, I can remember waking up to Eddie Williams's singing on school mornings in the 1950s and 1960s. "Hello, hello, hello . . . good morning, friends, and welcome to the *Eddie Williams Show*," were the lyrics to his cheery tune accompanied by the strum of chords and picked-out melody of his guitar. "I hope you're gonna stay tuned in to your radio . . . on the six-ten spot . . . upon your dial."

Hearing his voice through our dreams, half-awake, we listened for the sounds of our mother working in the kitchen. Drawers and cupboard doors opened and closed; water ran. The coffeepot began to perk on the stove; when we could smell the coffee upstairs and hear our mother and dad talking, we knew it was time to get up. Most of us. Our mom, Patsy, called up the stairs once or twice, for anyone who needed a little more motivation.

By the time we were dressed and downstairs she had a large saucepan of oatmeal ready, with a carton of milk out on the table, along with sugar, and often a box of raisins. Our dad ate a good-sized bowlful, toast, and sometimes a couple of eggs. He smiled at each child as we came into the kitchen.

"You kids look nice," he said, "you always look really nice." I know it gave him pleasure to see us getting ready for school; when I became a parent and had school-age children myself, I loved the sight of their clean faces and combed hair, their school clothes, and their backpacks.

We loved our mornings with Pat and Jerry. We were, as my sister Janet says, "happy, happy little kids," and our home life was like that of many others of the time. Our family was larger than most, but other than that we were not in any way unusual.

Except for one thing.

Patsy, early riser and champion of a good breakfast, regularly ate a cheeseburger for breakfast. That morning aroma of coffee and oatmeal, of eggs and toast, sometimes included the headiness (to some; I have never been a morning person, myself, and to me it was sometimes a little too much for early morning) of well-done beef; those busily optimistic morning sounds of coffee perking and Eddie Williams singing and talking sometimes included the sizzle of a hamburger patty frying in her smallest cast-iron pan.

Pat's breakfast sandwich was the hamburger patty with a slice of cheese between two slices of toast that

she cut corner to corner into triangles. She ate it standing, while she energetically helped us to get ready for
school; from time to time she took sips from her coffee
cup that she set down, as she moved, on the stove, on
the kitchen table, on a windowsill.

Our dad was a house painter and wore white dress
shirts to work in; we girls ironed a fresh one for him
every morning, as well as a pair of white painter's pants.
We took as much care with his work shirts as we did
with our school dresses; we wanted him to look nice,
too. I never minded ironing and still don't; I love the
smell of clean fabric rising in steam from the ironing
board.

I recall working the iron between shirt buttons to
make the shirt front lie nice and flat one morning, sa-
shaying slightly closer to the ironing board as Patsy
zipped past me with half a cheeseburger in one hand
and a hairbrush and rubber band in the other. Placing
the corner of the sandwich in her mouth she quickly
brushed our little sister Colleen's hair into a ponytail
that she secured with the rubber band. She sipped her
coffee, pulled up Jeanne's knee socks, smoothed the
skirt of her dress, and took another bite of cheeseburger.

"Did you eat?" she asked me. "Make sure you eat
something before you leave."

"I had some oatmeal," I answered.

"Are you still hungry? Do you want a bite of this?"

I shook my head. ("Noooooooooo.") "Why do you
eat those in the morning?"

In her answer I heard the joy she took in her household, in her large family, in her responsibilities, in life. "I've got a lot of work to do! This is full of protein; it gives me energy!"

She saw Jerry off to work in clean, ironed paint clothes, carrying his lunch pail; she waved her school-age children, dressed and fed a good breakfast, out the door. Then, I imagine, she settled down with her pre-schoolers, finished her cheeseburger, and had a second cup of coffee, listening to the six-ten spot on the radio dial.

The Exiles

*t*he Ojibwe word for woman is *ikwe* (ih-KWAY); the word for girl is *kwesens* (kway-ZAYNSS). In Ojibwe, adding a vowel and -*ns* to the end of a noun lets us know that it is small and precious. Kwesens is a small and precious woman. Through the teachings of our grandparents, which are the ways we try to keep today, we know that a little girl, a kwesens, will one day be a woman, an ikwe. She is of the sex that will carry and bring new life into the world. Because of this, women of all ages are regarded with honor. We are the physical anchor and spiritual link between past and present, and between present and future.

A teenage Ojibwe ikwe is an *oshinikwe* (osh-IN-ny-kway), a "new woman." She is not small anymore and is at the beginning of her womanhood; she is new. In the days that I was, myself, an oshinikwe, I was a student at Denfeld High School, the first of the fourteen

LeGarde children. If you attended Denfeld anytime between 1965 and 1988, you went to school with one of the LeGardes.

At Denfeld I played the French horn and learned to drive; I was introduced to the "Peer Gynt Suite" and the "1812 Overture" in world history class. The teacher, Mr. Gastler, also brought in movie reels of European refugees and other survivors of World War II; the black-and-white moving image of a young woman holding her hand over a barrel in which a fire was burning and warming her small child's feet with her hands still appears in my dreams. Kind and generous Mr. Strand, an English teacher, let us borrow books from his own eclectic and interesting collection of fiction paperbacks; another English teacher, Miss Endrizzi, taught us how to think critically, to read between the lines and to not take everything exactly as it was written.

We didn't study much about American Indians in high school; I can recall just one time that we did. In an English/humanities class I sat behind another Indian student, a tall young man with shoulders broad enough to hide behind. I enjoyed the anonymity of listening unseen, and the freedom to peek around his right shoulder when I wanted to watch what was going on. We had known each other since elementary school and regarded each other somewhat like relatives, which is of course what all Anishinaabeg are, in spirit and literally, too, from far, far back.

I thought that humanities class was very interesting: we studied art, theater, music, and literature, and through discussion and writing we connected the arts to social and historical events. It was in humanities class that we studied about American Indians, just that one time. On that day we watched *The Exiles,* a documentary about American Indians living in Phoenix around 1960.

Between 1953 and 1988, official federal Indian policy was called *Termination.* Goodness, what a word. What it meant was the ending of the United States Government's legal acknowledgment of American Indian tribes and, with that, those tribes' sovereign rights and individual members' identities. The Termination policy was implemented in various damaging ways. One of them, the Federal Relocation Program, involved the removal of young individuals and their families from home reservations and communities to large urban settings; some of these were Cleveland, Los Angeles, Seattle, Denver, Los Angeles, and Chicago. *The Exiles* was a documentary about American Indians who were exiles within their own homeland.

The lives of the people in the documentary were filled with hardships: unemployment, hunger, crowded and shockingly decrepit apartments, alcoholism, a complete social disconnect from the promises made by the Relocation Program workers. As the movie progressed, I heard in the semidarkness of drawn shades and turned-off lights some gasp, sigh, cluck their tongues; one or two snickered.

I perched forward to the edge of my chair, elbows on the desk and chin on my hands; ahead of me, the young man slid down in order that I might see better. We watched silently.

I can't recall the discussion after the movie, though I know it was brief. One student used the word *sexual* to

describe a young, pregnant Native woman, our honor
and hopes for the future rudely exposed and reduced to
a clinical term. Then it was time to write our individual
reactions. Head down, I looked at my paper, one red
vertical and twenty-four blue horizontal lines, on white
looseleaf with rounded corners, and began a sentence.

The young man turned around. "What are you going to write? What are you going to say?" he asked.

I showed him my paper. "Because I am an Indian,"
I had begun.

Although he clearly wanted to, he knew that a good
Anishinaabe doesn't tell others what to do. "You don't
have to . . ." was all he said.

During the time that she is still in her girlhood, an
oshinikwe is cared for, protected, perhaps even a little
spoiled; this is a part of Ojibwe child rearing. At the
same time she is being prepared for the time when she
will be an Anishinaabikwe. She observes, listens, thinks;
she begins to apply what she is learning to the world
outside Indian Country. She begins to practice drawing on the strengths of traditional Anishinaabe womanhood, in preparation for the tasks that will be hers when
she is a fully grown ikwe.

The first sentence was difficult, the second less so. I
wrote of sorrow and pride, of ambiguities and collid-
ing worlds. I wrote of my appreciation for having been
born an Indian. Of my parents' dreams for me and my
younger brothers and sisters.

When we passed our papers forward, the young man
ahead read mine quickly and nodded.

The Elders of Winter
and the Youth of Spring

*I*t is the custom at Ojibwe gatherings for elders to eat first, and for younger people to make sure that the older people are ahead of them in the food line. We are gently and regularly reminded of this right after the prayer of thanks. "We invite the elders to come up first," someone will announce. "Or if any elders would rather, please go ahead and sit down, and someone will bring you a plate of food."

The first time a young woman acknowledged me as an elder by bringing me a filled plate was at Vermilion, that eastern district of the Bois Forte Band of Ojibwe, and my reservation. At this particular feast my husband and I, being fairly new to the age of elderhood, thought that out of respect for those older and wiser than ourselves, we would just sit at a table at the back of the room and wait for the crowd to thin out.

"Do you smell turkey and gravy? Man, that smells

good; I'm pretty hungry," Tim said to me. Suddenly, a teenaged girl politely tapped my shoulder, smiled, straightened out the silverware that was in front of me on a lacy placemat, and set down a plateful of food. She asked if I would like coffee or some punch, if I might like a piece of pie. Then she paused, uncertain and a little flustered.

My hair silvered many years ago; my husband's did not. The young lady, who had been given the responsibility and honor of serving elders, had been instructed to fill plates with the nicest of food, arranged prettily, and present them to elders she saw sitting at the table. Tim's black hair and youthful looks confused her, but then her nice Ojibwe manners kicked in and she courteously directed the question to me: pointing her chin delicately toward my husband (or whoever she might have thought my non–elder-looking escort might be; I wonder what was going through her mind?), she asked in a lowered voice, "Does he want a plate, too?"

We still laugh about that, and we still remember the young lady's lovely manners.

Since then, we have been to many feasts and have been presented with plates of food by many young Native people, who consider it a privilege as well as a lot of fun to do that little task. As elders, our task is to reinforce this always-appropriate behavior, and so we always make sure to thank them, and to tell them how good the food looks. This, the ceremonial aspect of the presentation and acceptance of the gift of food, is an important part of passing Ojibwe traditions and values to the younger generation.

What do the young people learn as they serve the elders? They learn the power of intergenerational exchange. They learn to think of and serve others before themselves, that they are a part of a world that is larger than the individual, and they learn to have patience. (Will there be enough left of the cherry pie when it is their turn to eat? Perhaps not; in that case they experience the rewards of selflessness.) They experience the spiritual reinforcement and pleasure of being thanked and praised by the elders, who are the teachers of the people.

And we elders are gifted with much more than the food on the plate, lovingly selected and arranged, and sometimes overly generous in portion though it might be. We feel the honor of our years, and gratitude for all the time we have been given. Speaking with and accepting the plate of food dished up just for us by the young people who will be Elders themselves one day, we are energized and replenished. In the young people, those people of the spring season who carry plates, serve food, sweep floors, and clean up after the feast, we see our own parents and grandparents; we are reminded that life continues, and we are comforted.

I close here with a message to the young man, the ziigan-oshkii-inini, who at last year's spring powwow piled an extra spoonful of whipped cream onto Tim's apple crisp: you smiled, loped over to the coffee urn to refill our cups, told us to not bother with our dirty dishes, that you and the other kids would take care of things.

I know you will. Migwech.

LINDA LeGARDE GROVER is professor of American Indian studies at the University of Minnesota Duluth and a member of the Bois Forte Band of Ojibwe. She writes fiction, poetry, research articles, essays, and newspaper columns. Her short fiction collection *The Dance Boots* received the Flannery O'Connor Award and the Janet Heidinger Kafka Prize. Her novel *The Road Back to Sweetgrass* (Minnesota, 2014) received the Wordcraft Circle of Native Writers and Storytellers 2015 Fiction Award, and her poetry collection *The Sky Watched: Poems of Ojibwe Lives* won the Red Mountain Press Editor's Award. She lives in Onigamiising.